The God
of the New
Millennium

T0308523

First published by O Books, 2008
O Books is an imprint of John Hunt Publishing
Ltd., The Bothy, Deershot Lodge, Park Lane,
Ropley, Hants, SO24 0BE, UK
office1@o-books.net
www.o-books.net

Distribution in:

UK and Europe
Orca Book Services
orders@orcabookservices.co.uk
Tel: 01202 665432 Fax: 01202 666219 Int. code
(44)

USA and Canada
NBN
custserv@nbnbooks.com
Tel: 1 800 462 6420 Fax: 1 800 338 4550

Australia and New Zealand
Brumby Books
sales@brumbybooks.com.au
Tel: 61 3 9761 5535 Fax: 61 3 9761 7095

Far East (offices in Singapore, Thailand, Hong
Kong, Taiwan)
Pansing Distribution Pte Ltd
kemal@pansing.com
Tel: 65 6319 9939 Fax: 65 6462 5761

South Africa
Alternative Books
altbook@peterhyde.co.za
Tel: 021 555 4027 Fax: 021 447 1430

Text copyright Gregory Dark 2008

Design: Stuart Davies

ISBN: 978 1 84694 063 7

A CIP catalogue record for this book is available
from the British Library.

Printed and Bound in the UK

O Books operates a distinctive and ethical publishing philosophy in
all areas of its business, from its global network of authors to
production and worldwide distribution.
This book is produced on FSC certified stock, within ISO14001
standards. The printer plants sufficient trees each year through
the Woodland Trust to absorb the level of emitted carbon
in its production.

The God
of the New
Millennium

Gregory Dark

BOOKS

Winchester, UK
Washington, USA

To my sister:
In health inexorably Vicki; in sickness indeed Victoria.

ACKNOWLEDGEMENTS

I must start by thanking those I begin to consider indispensable to my work: Judith Browder, Bruce Crowther, Julian Day and Teresa Parrot.

The O-Books' team are (presumably) paid for their efforts. Nevertheless their general hand-holding and their specific indulgence of my technological dyslexia go way beyond the exigencies of professional courtesy. Thank you, my friends.

For their on-going support I also need to thank my nephew, Richard Larder, and – as ever – my daughter, Lyubov.

* * *

The 'mentor' is, for me, a difficult concept. Most of those who have profoundly affected my thinking I know only through their (mostly, written) work. However, those I have worked for have, without exception, taught me – not always in a positive way, but negative learning is also valuable.

Seven of my bosses (albeit for completely diverse reasons) were enormously influential: Edward Bond, John Cleese, Michael Codron, Graham Easton, William Gaskill, Gerald Thomas – and my father. To them possibly I owe a special debt of gratitude.

But to all those below I also owe considerably more than just a mention in a book! Some of these 'mentors' are, of course, dead. Their influence on me isn't. This list, I recognise, is incomplete. There are several of my employers, particularly those who used me on commercials or documentaries, whose faces I can see, but whose names (I'm afraid) elude me. I beg their pardon.

Dennis Abey, Alonso Alegria, James Allen, Juliet Alliston, Lindsay Anderson, Chris Auty, Julie Baines, Alan Berkinshaw, Michael Blakemore, Harry Booth, William Brayne, Ricou Browning, Chris Burt, Ken Campbell, Martin Campbell, Daniel Carillo, Robert Chetwyn, Bryan Coates, Sid Cole, Peter Collinson,

Kevin Connor, John Crome, Roger Croucher, Charles and Sheila Dark, Michael Deeley, Jane Deknetel, René Dupont, Ronald Eyre, Brian Farnham, John Frankau, Peter Gill, John Goldschmidt, Vance Goodwin, Fraser Heston, Adrian Hughes, Brian Izzard, Jill James, Ken Julian, Derek Kavanagh, Robert Kidd, Kris Klisowicz, Paul Knight, Ted Kotcheff, Barry Kulick, Verity Lambert, Milcho Malchevski, Erica Masters, Paul McCartney, Andrew McClaglen, Mike McGee, Raymond Menmuir, Bob Mercer, Helen Montagu, David Munroe, Gerard Oury, Douglas Pearce, Gerry Poulson, Tara Prem, Peter Rogers, Anthony Simmonds, Julia Smith, Ronnie Spencer, Jackie Stoller, Geoff Stott, Harry Alan Towers, Lindsey Vickers, Peter Wiles, Peter Willes, Roger Williams, Michael Winner, Scott Wodehouse, and Nicolas Wright.

'THE GOD OF THE NEW MILLENNIUM'

A search for balance in an age of spin

I knew you'd be late. You always are.

The lone bell of the lonely chapel had clanged its five cracked chimes. Goats were bleating on our hazy hillside. A dog barked at them, but more, I felt, from a sense of duty than with any energy.

I was gazing out to sea. My eyes are so feeble now, I don't know why I still come here. And yet I do. More often than you know. Here I feel closer to Arkona, knowing it was here he spoke for the last time, close to here that he said good-bye. I miss him, Sóphia. Quite a lot. Sometimes, gazing at the sea, there is communion with him.

And sometimes all there is, is gazing at the sea.

And in that gazing too there is communion with Arkona. And sometimes, yes, there isn't.

The rain had stopped by then. There was lushness in the green and bounce in the tufted grass. The smells were vibrant: of olives, citrus, almonds – the tang of sap. A breeze sighed through the reeds and whispered in the leaves. A brace of starlings warbled to each other, a solitary pigeon cooed its eerie dirge.

The ground had been softened by the rain. It muffled your approach. I was therefore lightly startled when I heard your voice. "I'm leaving the convent," you said. I think I was supposed to hear it as a statement of fact, of *inconsequential* fact. There was edge in the tone, though. And it fret-sawed through the veil.

The sun was directly behind you. It corona'd your wimple, haloing it – and you. I had to shield my eyes. The sun seems to smart my feeble eyes more than ever it did my strong ones. You looked beautiful. You always do. "You sound angry," I said. Wordlessly I invited you to sit down next to me. But you remained standing.

"Oh, I *am* angry," you replied. A tear ran down from your left eye. Those pigeon grey eyes that Arkona had so admired. Huffily you brushed away that tear, and stomped your foot, like a child, in exasperation. "I'm confused, angry … confused …" You seemed to want to continue with a list, but the words would not arrive.

"Confusion," I said aiming for lightness, "is chess for the uncompetitive."

"Not helpful," you returned sulkily.

"How about:" I said, I hope less frivolously, "'Confusion is a rite of passage for the curious'? For those seeking enlightenment, confusion is, by far, the biggest part of their journey. Order can only come *via* chaos, Sóphia. There is no other way. And there are no short cuts. *Only* via chaos, Sóphia. You live in an order. A monastic order. You know this."

"My confusion," you returned, almost as if confessing it, "is with God."

"Of course," I said.

"Of course?"

"You live in a convent. All who live in convents are confused about God."

"You think?"

"Doesn't the convent *encourage* you to be confused about God?"

You answered with a wry smile, "Not exactly, Lakshmi, no." Still your eyes were glowering, still your body was rigid with an anger feeding on itself, but there was now about the eyebrows a whisper of relief.

"Then," I said, "you are right to leave. You will never get closer to God in a place which tells you where, or who, God is."

"God is the question, right, not the answer? I mean, isn't that what Arkona said?"

"What Arkona did say was that for God to be God, God has to be *your* God. Don't let your God, Sóphia, be Arkona's."

"*My* God," you sighed. "That's such a big part of the problem."

"It's also a big problem. A big part of a big problem *is* something big. You seem to be berating yourself for calling a mammoth a mammoth."

You were, I think, about to snap back. You checked yourself, however, and hrrmphed a bitten tongue. Your eyes welled with tears, but you cast the iris heavenwards to stem the flow. I got the impression you'd done enough crying. You folded your arms across your breast. "I haven't got a God any longer," you said. "Or, probably what I should say, my God these days seems to be *three* gods."

"Not three," I said, probably rather too forcefully.

"Yes," you insisted, your nostrils starting to flare.

"Far more than three," I told you.

"*More* than three?" You seemed to be amazed.

And that's really the point of this little exercise – this doodling, maybe I should say. It's probably a silliness, probably no more than a sop to my vanity. But, talking to you, things seem to clarify in my mind. I hope they may for you as well. Whilst they're still fresh in that mind – I hope you won't object – I thought it might be an idea, jot them down.

Oh God, Sóphia, I know I'm not Arkona. Please don't ever feel you have to tell me that. I lack his poetry, lack the scale of his vision. My 'seeing', for a seeress, is remarkably limited. Even before my sight became so poor, my insight was very restricted. And my verbal talent is less. I will probably lack the courage even to show you this until I am dead. (If you see what I mean!) Even so, there are thoughts to which you encouraged me which I think are worth their thinking. And their mulling.

I know nothing. You know that. I have decided nothing. Like Arkona, it is not answers that I am even seeking. But it becomes tiresome always to write in the form of questions. Remember my tone. The page's punctuation may say statements. But if, Sóphia, you remember correctly the inflection in my voice you will hear only questions.

"*Far* more than three gods," I said. There was a slight pause before I continued, "The history of God, Sóphia, is not the history of religion."

"Which means?" you asked.

"God might or might not be manmade. Religion certainly is.

Don't look so alarmed. Hothouse flowers may have man's hand in them. They still wouldn't be possible without God. Man could not make *all* of God, nor could he make *everything* in religion. From where does it come, for instance, Man's ability to make God if not *from* God?"

"And that's not alarming, Lakshmi? For a good convent girl like me?"

"The truth is not alarming," I said. "It only becomes alarming when we make a bogeyman out of it, or allow it to be made into a bogeyman. God the bogeyman is certainly an invention made by Man.

"The history of God, Sóphia, it seems to me, is of the enlightened using metaphor in their quest to give insight into the inexplicable, to give form to the abstract. The history of so much *religion*, on the other hand, is of those considered – or claiming to be – God's conduits being ceded great earthly power, and the more venal of such conduits grasping for more. If you had such power," I asked you, "would you not think it best safeguarded by seducing the credulous into believing that only you could interpret the metaphor? Indeed, in some instances, even insisting that the metaphor *isn't* one?

"I believe it was the Egyptians who first proposed there was but one God – and that was from political, not metaphysical, motives. Previously the Egyptians had had a pantheon. As did, I think, all of the ancient civilisations – all, even, of the prehistoric tribes. Pantheons make sense."

"Go on," you said. You had calmed down sufficiently that you were now able to sit. You wrapped your knees in your arms, and allowed your eyes to settle on the cobalt, lightly choppy sea. Your gaze, however, seemed to be cocooned by my words. A young peasant strode past on the path above us.

"Even the Judaeo-Christian God," I continued, "recognises we will have more gods than one. What *is* a god, Sóphia, do you think?"

"Unknowable, no?" you returned. "Aren't we agreed on that?"

"I think many people would disagree with us. I think many people in your convent would disagree."

"Somewhat," you acknowledged with a smile.

"But because God is unknowable, does it also mean that *a* god is?"

"You're losing me," you said.

"Loath though I am to attach labels to God, just as an exercise, let's call God 'Life' – 'Life' in all its guises and manifestations, including the unknowable of life, and including the supernatural elements too, like the soul or the life-force or the afterlife: There can, after all, be no afterlife unless there is life."

"What in Oriental philosophies is called 'chi'," you suggested.

"Similar, certainly," I said. "How much wonder is there in Life, Sóphia? Don't you think our forefathers would have gazed in that wonder at the way, for instance, each year magically food would grow out of the ground?

"You know mankind's brightest being? The first person who, from her own observations, understood cause and effect: realised that if you put a seed into the ground, in six months time it would grow into food. She was probably also the most spiritual being of mankind. Because she must have had an inkling about the wonder, the miracle which is that process. If you're involved with something wonderful, something mysterious, don't you think it entirely feasible that you would start revering that … force, that impulsion, whatever it was? The force that was bringing about that miraculous transformation? Would you not want to know that force better? Would you not like to believe you could tap into it? Particularly, if your life depended on it?"

"Well, let's assume so for the moment," you conceded.

"In very short order, Sóphia, you create a pantheon. In fact, you create several. The god of food, for instance, one god of the supreme pantheon, would be the Zeus or the Wotan of its own: one which contained the gods of hunting and harvesting, say, of fire and water, of wine and festival and so forth."

"Yes," you again said hesitantly.

"Any Zeus is, of course, not only Zeus but includes within itself all the other gods as well. Zeus is not only parent to all these other gods, in other words, but also contains them."

"That I *can* see," you said.

"So much of the problem today is not with the gods in our pantheon – not even with the demons which all pantheons must inevitably also contain – but with the fact that we mistake subordinate gods for the important ones. We tend to venerate the oily rag and not the engineer. With our food, for example, we worship convenience not nutrition. And there is nothing wrong with convenience. But convenience is merely a cherub, whereas nutrition is a god indeed."

"The three Gods I have, though," you said, "they're *all* Zeus. They all *want* to be Zeus, anyway: the supremo, the numero uno. They're fighting in my head, the three of them, all of the time, all jockeying for position, all insisting it is *theirs*, the truth."

"And they all, of course, have truth within them."

"Of course, Lakshmi, they do. There wouldn't otherwise be a problem."

"I was being dense," I conceded. Well, I am a bit dense. There's no question about that. You're the one, Sóphia, with the brains.

We said nothing more for a while. I listened to the goats bleating and their bells clunking echolessly. Such a peaceful sound. I felt the sun ease into its evening torpor, and lay back on my elbows to bathe in its lazy warmth. You too were silent. On the outside. But from the inside of you I could hear the cacophony raging of strident voices, all yelling for attention, all seeking to outshout the others, all insisting they were truth, all demanding fealty and obedience. "Help me," you asked me quietly. So quietly I almost failed to hear it.

I was startled by the plea. "You have no need to ask," I said. "You know that."

"I had to hear myself say it," you replied.

"There are no answers," I said. "You know there are no answers."

"I do know, yes," you said. Your tone was struggling to appear as if it had surrendered to reality. But beneath that veneer I could hear the disappointment.

"We could look together for the questions," I suggested.

The distant bell clanged six times.

"Oh God, I'm late!" You sprang to your feet. And then, with a calm absent when you had asked me to help you, you added gently, "I'd like to talk some more."

"Good," I replied, as I rose and brushed the dust and dried grass from that awful tatty long brown skirt of mine. "Talk also with yourself, and with Arkona – and with God. Sometimes you will be talking to all three without even realising it."

"How do you talk to a question?" you asked, smiling.

I smiled back: "You just did," I said.

* * *

A month passed. It was warmer. The days were longer. I would have liked to have come later to the hillside. But I knew your convent hours were rigid. And I wanted to see you again. If I came later I might miss you.

Melancholy was, as usual, with me. Melancholy had become a companion. I had become comfortable with it. Latterly, though, my melancholy had been joined by a toddling loneliness. My communion was now not enough with Arkona, not even with God. My companionship with melancholy was not enough, the brush I had with other folk – Ulm and the olive farmer, the goatherd and my neighbour. My own children, as you know, live in very distant climes. The contact I have with my grandchildren is almost none. Saskja's independence was each day more determined. Rarely these days did she come to visit ...

I had stopped hoping you might return. Now I yearned for it.

Perhaps for that reason I heard your footsteps even before they had left the path. I could not let you know how glad I was to see you.

"I need a lover," you shouted from afar.

"So do I," I shouted back. I thought you were joking.

"What do you think, Lakshmi, do I leave the convent before I take one, or afterwards?"

I laughed awkwardly, uncertain about the seriousness of the question. "I should be angry with you," I said.

"Please don't be," you pleaded. "Everyone's angry with me. After our last talk I was late back. The abbess was angry with me. I was forbidden to leave the grounds until today. I was told to make good use of my time. I did so by thoroughly getting on everyone's nerves. That's using time wisely, wouldn't you say?"

I said nothing, but my insides sizzled in a grin. I realised I'd been afraid somehow I'd driven you away. Being forbidden to leave the convent threw your absence into a different light. You don't yet know how important you are to me. And, I'm sure unaware of the feelings churning through me, you trilled on happily, "When she first confined me, the abbess, I dreamt up the idea of a lover to revenge myself on her. How better, after all, to enrage her? But then I realised, I hadn't dreamt up the idea of a lover for that reason at all. Vengeance may have been the icing, but the cake was the lover. And, what's more, I realised I didn't need to justify my desire for a lover – probably my *need* for one.

"Our first truck with the divine, you said, was of gods in a pantheon. You talked about the wonder Man had in a seed growing. How much wonder must Man have had, then, in sex? Surely, in Man's first pantheon, Eros just had to have had a place – a pretty prominent one, too. Well, Lakshmi, it occurred to me: I'm as much a child of evolution as anyone else. I want sex in my pantheon too."

I know you can't cross a chasm in two leaps. The length of your vault nevertheless astounded me: In the space of a month, you'd gone from an arcane theological conundrum, to craving that pleasure most forbidden to nuns. "Right," I said, something – *anything* – just to make a noise.

"Thank you, Lakshmi," you said, with a big sigh, bending

towards me, your hands clasped gently together.

I wondered what I had done to have warranted thanks. "You talked about miracles. You talked about our forefathers creating gods out of that which they didn't understand – a seed, you said, germinating into grain.

"And you're right. Of course you're right. There were gods too, weren't there, for thunder and lightning? And I can see why. I'm often frightened in storms. And *I* know what they are. (Or, maybe what I should say, I was told what they are which I've now forgotten.) But I can certainly imagine early Man believing a thunderstorm was an indication that some supernatural power – God before God had a name – was angry with him, and that that supernatural power somehow had to be appeased."

"It's good to see you again," I said very quietly. You didn't hear me.

"Sorry, Lakshmi, I'm chattering away nineteen to the dozen. Like a Trappist finally allowed to speak." You knelt behind me, squeezed your arms around my shoulders. It made me wince. You didn't see it made me wince. "I've been thinking, see, since our last meeting," you continued. "Doing a lot of it, thinking. Doing a lot of feeling too. I found myself … in the shower …" You were still squatting behind me, still with your arms around me. And I was still wincing. It was so painful. You buried your face in the nape of my neck – both embarrassed, and eager to share a secret. "My hands suddenly became a man's hands. I was being touched by a man's hands and my hands were telling my brain what a man would be feeling touching me. It was electric, Lakshmi. And it was very powerful. I couldn't rid myself of the sensation. At each service I sought to immerse myself in what I liked to think was the 'spiritual', sought to give myself over to the divine, and I found myself instead overpowered by those man's hands and by the feeling of those man's hands on me and by the feeling that feeling invoked.

"I suddenly thought, if Life is the president of the pantheon, then somewhere in the senior Cabinet there is also sex."

"There's no doubt of that," I agreed.

"It was sex I wanted, Lakshmi – it *is* sex – more than love. It was Shakespeare's Cleopatra, wasn't it, who had immortal longings in her? Well, in me, there were what my Church would call 'immoral' longings, except that I didn't find anything immoral about my longings at all. I've never felt more pure in my life, nor – paradoxically – more chaste."

"Of course you wanted sex. You are intelligent and thus curious. You have had experience of love. You have had no experience of sex."

"Of course I have," you chortled.

"*Of course* you have?" I asked.

"Sex is not only the act of sex, the consummation of sex."

"Except," I said, "if you're an American president."

"Sex is a god."

"Of course," I said, "sex is a god. It is, in fact, the god with the most identities, with the most manifestations, with the most complexities. Probably with the most power. Which is why, maybe, religions have sought to sully it."

"And sex, in humans, *is* about sex," you suggested. "Otherwise women would die in menopause."

"Or they would, at least," I agreed, "stop being sexually active."

"You mean," you ventured, "you still …?" I suppose you hoped your blushing would finish the question for you.

"Well, not a lot recently," I confessed. "But that doesn't mean, us crones, we don't have yearnings too. I'm told we are unique amongst mammals in that regard."

"Okay," you said, a touch coyly.

"And from it, Sóphia, we can only draw one conclusion: that whilst, in evolutionary terms, procreation may have been the principle reason for sex, it is not the only one." You suddenly became aware of a brace of flies buzzing around your nose, and started shooing them away. "And that," I continued, "smashes all those killjoy theories of too many Churches, and their condemnation of contraception or homosexuality or anything else. This condemnation is thus clearly not God-made. I don't even think it's manmade: It's *priest*-made."

You looked at me, somewhat askance. I remembered that you'd been in convents most of your adult life, that habits are not broken with one blow. I wanted your friendship. I was desperate for it. And for your company. I felt I needed to appease you. So I quickly added, "Oh, just ignore me, Sóphia. I really don't know what I'm talking about. I get so muddled. And about so many things." Well, that part was true, anyway. I do often get muddled.

You were still looking at me somewhat askance, but you said, "That's gratifying."

"Don't be gratified by that," I advised you. "I am a stupid old woman. That I am confused is probably due mostly to stupidity and age. But please be gratified by this: Confusion in the bright – and you *are* bright, Sóphia, far from being a measure of ignorance, is one of intelligence.

"Ignorance is blissful because it is questionless. Not only does it not know enough to know which questions to ask, it knows so little it doesn't think there are any. Start to acquire wisdom, you have to acquire questions. The greater the wisdom, the more questions, and the more interconnected those questions: the greater the wisdom, in other words, the greater the confusion.

"Be gratified also by this: Usually you arrive at the right questions only via the wrong ones. My field of expertise is extremely narrow," I said, "but in one thing I know myself to be expert: asking the wrong questions."

"Is it a wrong question to ask if I should take a lover?"

"*I* can't answer that, if that's what you mean."

"Not 'should I take a lover', just 'is it a wrong question?'"

"Oh, I *can* tell you, you should take a lover."

"I should?"

"What I can't answer is whether that's a wrong question."

"I should take a lover?"

"Of course you should take a lover, Sóphia."

"Unless?" you asked, voicing the word I had left dangling in the pause.

"Unless you feel you shouldn't," I smiled.

And then you let go of my shoulders, and you did see me wince. You asked what was wrong, and I told you about this rheumaticky pain which has started. You made me promise I'd have it looked at.

I smiled again. More amply. You said no more. And neither did I.

* * *

This time it was more than a month. I knew I wasn't well. To get up the hillside now required an effort – and of will – I was not used to. Still my weakening eyes would gaze out to sea. There was, though, less communion with Arkona, and such as it was was shallower. My thoughts rather would saunter to you, to wondering how you were or what you might be doing … to wondering when it would be that I would see you again.

A storm was coming, perhaps a gale. The heat nestled in the olive trees like leaded leaves, and piggy-backed my shoulders like a wriggly and cranky toddler. The wildlife sought shelter, and I myself considered taking refuge in the little chapel. Though 'taking refuge' is perhaps not the right expression. Ulm, its priest, is such a nice and gentle man. The weather doesn't need to be bad for me to speak to him. Often I do. He too was there the last time Arkona spoke.

The goats were already being returned to their overnight pasture. There was now urgency in the dogs' barking at them, and a certain sogginess already audible in the clunk of their bells. It was crazy for me to be here. Almost defiantly I stared out to sea, challenging the elements to do their worst … but also entreating God to let me feel better. Canute, if you like, on an each-way bet!

I heard your sandals crack the brittle earth. My back was turned to the path. I had no way of knowing they were your sandals, even that they were a woman's – and yet I did. Without any doubt at all. "Sóphia?" I asked.

"Giselle," you replied.

"Giselle? What does that mean?" I asked.

"I left the convent," you told me as you approached. You were sucking on a straw of marsh grass. Your mood was far more contemplative than the words that came from you. "I got my name back. Giselle is my own name. Not the best swap in the world, I grant you. My parents were ballet fans. I think they thought if I could cope with Giselle I could cope with anything else. I also got my dowry back. I rented a small apartment. And found work in the hospital. And I'm in love, Lakshmi. Well, not exactly in love. Not what I think novelists would describe as love. I haven't even met the man. But I have seen him. From afar. I think I've picked my first lover. You know, do you, it's about to rain? About to pour, I should say."

"You don't sound angry," I commented. "The last time we spoke, you sounded angry."

"No room for anger," you replied. "Not even confusion. I've got the bit between my teeth, Lakshmi ...," before you added with a giggle, "... and an itch between my legs. How can God be God if the veneration of God requires so much dreariness? So much misery?"

"Why does it have to?"

"That's a right question."

"This, I hope, is another."

"Go on," you said.

"Why does God have to remain a constant?"

"Yes, that too is a right question."

"Could God not one day be the search for God, and the next day be the discovery?"

"*Can* you discover God? Wouldn't your opinion be, that the discovery of God would be the dissolution of God?"

"On Wednesday, perhaps. But perhaps on Thursday I might think differently," I replied.

"Just as, I suppose, if I discover God on Thursday, on Friday I might have to start the search again."

"Are you confused today?" I asked.

"I'm sure I am," you said. "It's just that the confusion is overwhelmed."

"So today your God is one you absorb, rather than one you aspire to know better. These too are gods, Giselle. And these gods too are part of the pantheon ..."

"And part of God."

"Obviously, and part of God," I repeated. "Maybe even part of three gods."

"I think the nuns were glad to see the back of me, to tell you the truth. I think they were getting fed up with my problems. They've certainly had it with my gods. Yes, Lakshmi, still the three of them."

"Do they have identities, these gods? I won't say names, but is there any kind of handle you can put on them?"

"Sort of," you replied. You threw away the straw you had been sucking and pulled out another long shaft, I remember, and started rolling it between your fingers. "There's the God of my Church, that's one. The God, I should probably say," you added hastily, "of what I no longer know *is* my Church. Or, even more what I should probably say, the God of what I no longer know is my Church which I no longer know is my God."

"And the second?" I asked.

"Is the God Arkona urged me to find, *my* God. Though that God eludes me as yet. Oh, I have a sense of it. But I'm taking it on trust that the search will reap some reward."

"You have considered, have you, that the reward may be the search itself?"

"I was rather hoping it might be more," you smiled lightly. You lay back on your elbows. "It has occurred to me that my God might be the *search* for God."

"For many people it is," I told you. "And most of those for whom God is the search for God, aren't aware that, for them, that is what God is. For many others, God is the *belief* in God. Most of those don't know that either. And the God even of the most religiously orthodox must include the search for and belief in God, so for even the most orthodox those two gods are a *part* of their God."

You seemed to hear that. You seemed to consider it. But, before you could comment on it, you exclaimed, "Look at that cloud. It's huge, Lakshmi, and hugely black and it's *stampeding* its way towards us. Let's get to somewhere dry."

You stood and offered me your hand. You've often done that. But previously your help had been, more than anything else, a courtesy. This time there was real effort required to get me to my feet. And I couldn't disguise the pain there was in my shoulder. You asked about my appointment. I reminded you I'd be going next week.

"The third?" I asked, as we were walking. You didn't understand. "Your third god?" I asked.

"Right. The third god, Lakshmi, is the … what is it? Force, I suppose, … dynamic … dynamo that runs the world. The God of what appears to me to be this ever more godless world."

"And that worries you, that paradox?" I asked, like an idiot. "You don't think God must also incorporate godlessness?"

"Of course God must incorporate godlessness," you returned sharply. The rain was now beginning to splatter onto the baked ground. It was still shingly, the rain; was not yet the boulders it would soon become. "It's not the paradox which concerns me, it's the convenience that paradox provides:" you continued, "to square all the metaphysical circles, to justify all the abuses."

"I'm being dense again, I'm sure," I said, "but ..." I shrugged. I couldn't see what you were trying to drive at.

"It seems to me," you said, "everything in Nature is curved. Man didn't 'invent' the wheel, he discovered it. The wheel is all around him. Man's only invention, it seems to me, is the straight line. There are no precedents for it in Nature, Lakshmi, nothing in Nature that is elemental to it – as, let's say, microwaves are to the mobile phone."

The rain was starting to beat heavily. It wasn't only soaking, it was also bruising us. You were urging a pace that I simply couldn't maintain. At the same time, you carried on talking.

"Man always believed time was linear," you said. "Well, Einstein saw that belief off. Likewise, Man's thinking, Man's understanding and philosophy tend all to be linear. And thus logic. Logic does lead to truth, of course it does. It leads rather to *a* truth, that's what I should probably say. I suspect, though, that man's truth is a synthetic, a man*made* truth. Which doesn't make it less truthful, but it does limit it.

"God's truth or Nature's truth, or – to use your term, Lakshmi – Life's truth is likely to bend, to be wavy. If it bends, then sometimes it just must bend back on itself and therefore, going out, meet itself coming back. Paradox thus is inevitable."

"Well, so logic, at least, would dictate," I said, teasing you, I hope gently.

"Paradoxically enough," you teased me back. God, how I wanted, how I desperately wanted, to get in from that rain. Streams were running down my face, my hands were turning blue. And on my back each falling drop felt like grape-shot made of ice. "It's just too convenient, though, isn't it?" you said. "*Way* too convenient, I mean. It allows the circle so neatly to be squared, so effortlessly: the contradiction, for example, between a merciful and a vengeful God."

"You cannot square a circle," I suggested to you, lifting a sodden corner of my shawl. "A squared circle is a square. Likewise an explained God or an understood God is *that*. It has changed form, and thus it cannot be the same god God was before you explained or understood God. Which, for me, means it can't *be* God."

"Everything is immeasurable because the act of measuring distorts what it is you are measuring?"

"Something, a theory, which has little import except in an abstract context. But there its meaning can be extremely significant."

"And not significant at all?" you suggested.

"Yes." Despite my discomfort, I laughed. "And not significant at all."

* * *

The chapel is extraordinary. You know that. Tiny. A matchbox chapel. No cathedral in the world, however, no mosque, pagoda, synagogue or temple hosannas God's glory more loudly or with greater beauty. It is the Hallelujah Chorus sung by mutes, the fly-past of ostriches. The roughcast is *infused* with grace, the cheap whitewash distempered with holy water, the floor of rocks Axminstered with charity, the unvarnished benches that are the pews, the tiny altar, all suffused with an awe that is unawesome. And therefore truly holy.

Now it *was* boulders of rain which tumbled from the sky. It was almost black outside. Through one of the windows, though, beamed a shaft of light that luminesced like a triangulated halo. As we entered we were both enamelled by this aura and were awash with it. Any testiness or heaviness there might have been was lifted from us as if they were coats taken by hat-check seraphim.

"Never have I seen this place more beautiful," you said, in reverential whisper.

"Your three gods?" I asked, rubbing my soaking hair with my equally soaking shawl.

"Yes?" you said, your fingers spatulaing the water from your dripping brow.

Forlornly I was wringing out my shawl. "The Gods, you said: the first of your Church, the second the God Who is yours, and the third Who is the world's dynamo?"

"Yes?" you said again, finger-combing your hair.

"You don't think, do you, that's what Christians might mean by the Father, the Son and the Holy Ghost?"

"No."

"You don't think that too might be a metaphor?"

"They think Christ is the Son of God, Lakshmi."

"This is a Church which represents the body of Christ with bread and wine."

"They still think Christ is – unmetaphorically – the Son of God."

"And it's not possible, Giselle, the Christ Himself used Himself as a metaphor?"

"I'm going to say 'go on'," you said slowly, "but I'm not sure I entirely mean it."

"Just examine the possibility, Sóphia. That's all we're doing, examining possibilities."

"Giselle," you reminded me. "That 'possibility', as you call it, it's a big lump to swallow, Lakshmi. Even the examination of that possibility, it's a *huge* lump to swallow. It might take some adjustment."

"If the God of your Church, let's say, were the original God, the metaphysical, the unknowable God, that God would be the Father."

"Yes," you said, with some reluctance.

"Siring your personal God, the One personal to you, which is the Son."

"And the Holy Ghost?"

"Is the God manifested in the spirit in which we are encouraged to live our daily lives – and in the manner we are *allowed* to live it. The God, if you like, which impels the world, which motivates it: the God, as you put it, of a godless world."

"And those three gods would then all include at least parts of each other, of course," you said, "which would go some way to explaining the other Christian concept of Three in One, and One in Three."

"Without resolving the mystery."

"And God the Father would then be Faith, God the Son Hope and the Holy Ghost Charity?" you mused, mostly to yourself.

"A Holy Ghost," I said, " Who is *no longer* Charity."

"And maybe, Lakshmi, therein lies the world's central problem."

Ulm had been seated throughout this time at the wall end of one of the benches, invisible in the shadows. "You should have come in ten minutes ago," he said to both of us, still in his lair. Have you ever noticed how his toothlessness causes him to lisp a little, to struggle with his 'b's and 'd's? We both jumped a little. "Do you need to pray?" he asked, oblivious of the startle he had caused. "If you need peace, I shall leave you."

"To pray in such a place, Ulm, is almost tautologous," you said. "Inside this chapel I feel that I am inside a prayer."

"Then I'll leave you in peace to be within that prayer," said Ulm. "To be one with God. Even to be one with three gods."

You looked surprised. Maybe even affronted. You thought the two of us, we had been talking in confidence. Ulm came out of the shadows. Stroked by the light, his walnut face looked more wizened and wrinkled than ever. In his eyes there was a concern for you, tempered by wry amusement: the parent reassuring the nightmared child that the wicked witch does not exist. "Don't be angry with me," he pleaded with you. "I couldn't help but overhear. I've been a priest for over forty years. I've had problems with God for over fifty."

"I know mystery should be allowed to be mystery. And I try to allow it to be," you told him, your tone still dusted with a sprinkle of rebuke, "but it's like a wobbly tooth – you can't leave it alone. *I* can't, I should probably say."

"She's also going to take a lover," I 'joked'. But it wasn't a joke, it was an announcement in banner headlines. It was enormously indiscreet, and I apologise. I'm not even sure I know where it came from, the 'joke'. Clearly, at some level I wanted to hurt you. Maybe so that you felt my hurt. The ache in my shoulder-blades had suddenly become a full-fledged pain. I think I was trying to blame that, at least in part, to your pulling me up. Pain seems to require us to blame someone for it. Maybe that's why in problematic families the most common role cast is that of the scapegoat. That's no excuse. I don't tender it as one. What I do tender, again, is an apology.

I sat down, I remember, on the bench. Tried to snuggle into the shadow that Ulm had just left.

"Life is a miracle," he said. I had the feeling it was only *ostensibly* to you. "Man is also a miracle. Both are confined by the carnal, and defined by it. It bemuses me, if God is an essential element in the creation of life – and if God *is* God, how can God not be? – how can you venerate God without venerating the carnal?"

"Heavens, Ulm, I'm not worried about taking a lover," you told him.

"Oh, good," said Ulm, not without disappointment. You weren't shocked! He was used to shocking a congregation. I think he enjoyed shocking them. Maybe he was still trying to shock you when he added, almost to himself, "Sadly, when I finally arrived at that conclusion, I was too old to do anything about it."

But that too you let pass without shock, indeed without comment. Instead, you said, "It's not even any longer, the problem, that of my having three Gods. Well, it is, but it's more defining what in those Gods *is* God, and what is Man: the strictures that are divine, and those that are synthetic."

"The strictures of the scriptures?" asked Ulm, his face inscrutable. And then he cackled. That wonderful, infectious laugh of his, part imp, part guardian angel. And we couldn't help ourselves, we laughed too.

Ulm looked up at the leaking roof. "Also paved with good intentions," he said enigmatically, "is the *priests'* road to Hell.

"Most priests, like most politicians," he said, "start out wanting the best for their congregation, wanting to do their best by them. But priests and politicians both get corrupted."

The rain at that stage was hammering on the tiled roof; already rivulets were teeming through where tiles were missing. Waiting for this contingency was a motley of buckets, pans and dishes. With the aplomb of habit, Ulm set these beneath the drips.

"And in the best of us," he went on, "our corruption emanates usually from a very similar source: We think we cannot express doubt; that doubt will disturb those who hear it; that it will disorientate them. We would be failing in our duty, we tell ourselves, if we were to allow those who listen to us to hear our doubt." Once you'd noticed what he was doing, you leapt to your feet and started to help. But this broke the habit, and the aplomb was left floundering.

Ulm continued, "There is, of course, a huge arrogance nestling in those thoughts. But for all its arrogance, the motive can be pure. Usually it isn't, sadly. Usually it's to do with the priests' and politicians' laziness, their own comfort, their spiritual indifference or diffidence. But it *can* be pure. And we lose little by conceding them purity – *even* when such flouts the evidence."

If I'd been feeling better I'd have argued that last point, but I let it pass. I suspect for too long we have tried to ascribe noble motives to those who seek power over us. I think today we have to start questioning all their motives – and ours. And all of the time.

"For most of my life," Ulm continued, "I have been trying to discover what prayer is. Have I ever let my congregation know? Only, if I'm honest, indirectly and obliquely."

"Do you know now? What prayer is?" you asked him directly.

He looked at you for a moment, deciding, I think, whether or not you were somehow mocking him. "I'm coming to the conclusion," he said, "fundamentally it's only two things: It's an act of humility which helps us to remain right-sized; and it's the tapping into whatever it is, the metaphysical force out there. That 'tapping into' isn't God, any more than the switch is electricity. But, just as you cannot access electricity *without* the switch, so you cannot tap into the supernatural without prayer."

"You think God is only there if you *want* God to be there?" you asked. A right question, I thought. A *good* question. I was massaging my shoulder (as best as I could), looking fretfully up at the leaking roof, praying for some relief to this awful ache. There was, I thought, also *that* element to prayer. sometimes it is all that remains to us. It is our last desperate hope. Why, then, I wondered, is it usually so unsuccessful? In my experience of prayer, the more I have needed some kind of divine intervention, the less forthcoming it has been. A bit like a bus, really: the more tired I am, the longer I have to wait for one.

Ulm considered what you said for a moment or two. "Maybe the act of prayer makes you more aware of God's presence," he suggested, "able therefore to avail yourself that much more of God's power." And maybe not, I thought to myself. But I stayed in the shadows and said nothing – I ...if you like ... skulked in my sulks!

Though he tried to hide it, Ulm resented your help with the drip-catchers more than he welcomed it. I make this point only because it's something I so often forget. I think because I offer help, people want it. I think because I have helped, people are grateful for it. It's not necessarily the case. Indeed it is even rarely the case.

"Ritual is important for us, as a species," Ulm prattled on. "The ritual of prayer no less than the ritual of rites of passage. Indeed, even in our secular today, rites of passage are usually seasoned with prayer." Covertly he was still louring at you for your help, but he was also (I could see) resenting his resentment. "It is, prayer, something else which would seem to distinguish us in the animal world. 'Seem to' because we have no idea what passes through an animal's mind, and to think that prayer is an articulation of prayer is to misunderstand it. Which is not to say, that its articulation is not a completely acceptable form of prayer; nor that it is not one of the functions of Man's prayers to supply, if you like, verbal totems.

"Another part of Man's prayer – of course it is – is superstition. But it would be a brave man who ventured to suggest where superstition ends and the supernatural begins.

"It would also be a brave man who came to a firm conclusion about which came first, prayer or God. Priests or prayer: is that chicken and egg? Lakshmi likes good questions. 'Right' ones, as she calls them. Here's one for you: Were priests discovered or invented?"

"That is a right question," I agreed. I wanted to be home, and in the dry and warm, preferably snuggled under the bedclothes.

"That is yet another answer," Ulm continued, "that we'll never know. Probably there was an element of both. Both were certainly interdependent, the discovery of priests and their invention.

"Make no mistake about it, those dilemmas do matter. Because if we knew where the various dividing lines were, it would be easier to define what of social cohesion was innate, what invented by primitive man, and what was wreaked through what was claimed to be divine exhortation. In other words, to answer your questions, Giselle, about what is God-made and what made by Man – and if not to answer them totally, then at least to start to answer them."

The rain seemed to be easing off. Or was that my imagination? You were immersed in Ulm's words. I hope what you were doing was not simply accepting them, but considering them. Like all wise men, Ulm can sometimes talk total nonsense.

"It is a frequent debate today," he continued, "the relative importance of nature and nurture. Priests and politicians shy away from the debate. I suspect because it is too challenging. But by that reticence we do a huge disservice to those we portend to serve. Politicians need to encourage that debate because it is so important to mankind's future. And we priests need to address it because it is so important to mankind's past. And today's mankind needs to insist we do because both future and past are so important to the present – *its* present, and, Giselle, yours.

"We can't possibly *know*. Not any of this. Everything's now so mixed up – creed with myth, belief with legend, superstition with religion – we can't possibly *know* where it all started, any of it: faith, religion, the abuse of religion. We can only surmise." He walked over to you and took a couple of the drip-catchers from you.

"What is religion, if not legend coupled with faith?" I asked.

Instead of replying, Ulm quizzed you, "Have you ever asked anyone to pass on a message?" He bent down to place a blue bucket under a meandering trickle.

As if to a really stupid question you replied, "Yes."

"Ever had one passed on correctly?" He paused for a moment

or two. He set down another of his drip-catchers. "And we're not dealing here with a single message being passed on *once*. We're dealing with a whole canon of legend, an entire history being told and retold, in Chinese whispers, over millennia.

"The story-tellers' priority has never been with accuracy. Always the audience's interest has taken precedence. 'Telling stories' has even become a synonym for telling lies. And that was the case long before twentieth century journalists were famously exhorted never to let the truth interfere with a good story.

"Maybe it was even then that mankind sealed its doom. Maybe that's one of the tragedies of Man – his inability to resist spinning a yarn. We all do it – we're all in our ways anglers describing the one that got away. All of us, we all tend to aggrandise our achievements, and overstate the odds against us. It's normal, it's human."

"I suppose I do that too," you said with rather more reluctance than I would have expected. You glanced at me, but didn't really see me. The shadow I had chosen was doing a good job of shielding me. Despite my best endeavours, I knew the pain was beginning to register on my face.

"Did priests, having been invented or discovered, devise the idea of an omnipotent God? Wouldn't their kudos be enhanced the greater the power wielded by the force they were representing? To have the ear of something all-powerful makes you more powerful than to have the ear of something with limited power. And didn't priests thus start to rule through fear? And isn't that precisely what politicians learnt from them? And is that not exactly how they still govern? Through fear?"

"Government does seem to contain that element," you conceded.

"Us priests, we compounded fear with sex."

"Sex?" you asked.

"The carrot to mollify the stick of fear."

"Sex?" you asked again.

Ulm smiled. He'd caused the shock he wanted. "I suspect priests, shortly after we became priests – and I suspect with even more certainty that many of my colleagues will wish me ill for saying this –, were (not to put too fine a point on it) in the rhino-horn business."

"Excuse me?" you asked, not exactly stunned, but closer to it than I suspect you'd liked to have been. Ulm hid his glee beneath a deeply-lined sanguinity. One of the extremely few advantages of aging is that wrinkles provide such very good cover.

Sanguinely, he continued, "Probably Man's first god was to do with food – a god of hunting, probably, or foraging. Way before he thought of growing crops. I'd be prepared to wager, though, that shortly after the birth of Man's first god, there arrived the *scapegoat* god. The god whom man, the gender, could blame for a lack of prey or a lack of berries, a god whose capriciousness would exonerate him sufficiently that woman would not withhold her sexual favours. And, with one mighty leap, at that moment we priests entered the rhino-horn business.

"We all know the profits there are in that trade. The antediluvian price, I suspect, was not gold but veneration. In exchange for sex, priests were endowed with wisdom, with the ability to interpret God's mysteries in ways that 'lesser' mortals couldn't.

"Shortly thereafter – again I'd be prepared to wager – priests sought to control man's sexual behaviour. Couple that control with their (the priests') exclusive communion with a Supreme Power, and those priests could manipulate the *whole* of man's behaviour. Priests, in other words, were in politics aeons before politics was ever thought of."

"*And* in the rhino-horn business!" you added, with a smile. The storm, thank God, *was* starting to ease. What had been the deluge through the roof now was just the outflow of a tap.

"And in the rhino-horn business," Ulm confirmed, matching your smile.

"Sex and politics, what an unlikely combination!" I commented.

"La plus ça change," you added.

"I'm sorry," I said. "I have to go home. Even if I get soaked, I have to know that I'm on my way home."

"It's that shoulder of yours, isn't it?" you asked. "You've got to have it looked at, Lakshmi. That's not a friend telling you, that's a nurse." I withered a look at you. That comment was not for my benefit, but Ulm's. The two of *us*, already we knew I'd made an appointment.

"We'll walk together," suggested Ulm. "Get soaked together, know together, Lakshmi, you are on your way home."

* * *

It was a struggle getting to the bus-stop. The path had become a rink of mud, and we skidded along it more than we walked. Ulm held one of my arms and you the other. As is the way with most of us who spend a lot of time alone, Ulm, having started to talk, was not about simply to shut up.

"When politicians today berate priests for meddling in the affairs of state," he said, "they should realise it is they who are the interlopers, the gate-crashers, not the other way around."

"That doesn't help me much," you said. "In defining, I mean, what belongs to whom. What, in Christ's words, is God's, what is Caesar's."

"The problem has been that for so long Caesar has not only claimed what *is* his, but what is God's as well," said Ulm. "And too many of us priests have been complicit in that. We have allowed Caesar to claim God's authority, and to insist we can only render unto God *via* Caesar.

"If Lakshmi is right, and if the Trinity is a metaphor for the three elements of God which she describes, there is an overlap between Father and Holy Ghost. An inevitable, and an original overlap. Which is, as you said, part of the Three in One and One in Three. But too many Caesars – and too many priests – have aggravated that overlap until it has become an impenetrable jumble.

"Mankind stands on an abyss today. You would think it was expecting some kind of divine intervention. It's not going to happen. God's not going to suddenly break the habit of several billion years, reveal Himself to us and save us like some kind of Clark Kent of the universe. Why should He? There's a huge universe out there. Not even on this planet will life die. *Human* life may. Too much of animal life along with us. But life itself *will* continue. I understand there's time still for another evolutionary process before whatever life takes our place needs to flee to Mars. Or the life that succeeds us will adapt to living in hotter climes."

We finally arrived on the paved lane. I was relieved. Our shoes were all caked with mud, like Australian crocodiles caught in a drought. My shoulder felt as if it were being prodded with a flaming poker. I felt hunched and broken, an old biddy hobbling to her grave. I also felt you were not so much holding my arms as holding me up. I thought at the time that Ulm's continued monologue was a further example, as if one were needed!, of male insensitivity. But I think now – now that I am again warm and dry and the pain in my shoulder is at least bearable – that it was his way of getting me home. If he'd allowed me respite to complain, I might have had to stop somewhere on the way.

"If mankind is to survive, then mankind needs to make a commitment to survive," he said. "Part of that commitment is to recognise that many who now govern us are leading us not to any Promised Land, but to Armageddon. And part of that commitment consists of deciding what *is* Caesar's and what is, in fact, God's. What is the Father's, and what that of the Holy Ghost.

"There are plenty of people who would call themselves 'atheist' who look in wonder at the loping of a giraffe or the pigeon-toed lolloping of a polar-bear. Personally, I wonder how many of such people are indeed atheists, and how many mistake atheism for disliking or disbelieving in the God, or gods, of religion. For me, anyone who appreciates wonder or beauty or who recognises the importance of life is communing with spirit. Once you commune with spirit, the divine has entered your life. And thus God. I suppose that's by-the-bye, but, you know, I'm never sure what *is* by-the-bye. Or that anything is.

"God is blamed for a whole panoply of things that have nothing to do with God – many of today's so-called 'acts of God' are acts of Man's arrogance. Hurricane Katrina may not have started without God, but it would not have had the force it did without Man's complicity, nor wreak the devastation it did without Man's negligence."

* * *

The bus was new and cream-coloured. It had power-steering. It was articulated. Posh. The Orphalese council glowed in its pride of it, and the driver himself beaconed. It was able to snake around the narrow cobbled Orphalese streets with a sleakness that was almost oily. The driver did not exactly prohibit the conveyance of goats, but such was most sternly not encouraged. Nor that of any livestock. Even passengers were tolerated only under sufferance. Passengers used seats, smeared hand-rails, walked on the shiny floor, gazed out of the polished windows. Passengers could sully the pristine, make scratches, dents, *stains*.

The driver was so small he could only just be seen above the steering wheel. He had the face of an over-ripe tomato and the hair of a brilliantined Valentino. But his heart was huge. And his heart belonged entirely to his bus.

You made a dive, Giselle, for an empty seat and grappled it like an anchor seeking purchase on a bed of stainless steel. You claimed your prize by sitting on it. And there you waited until, wan and wasted, I sidled to join you. You ceded the seat. I flopped into it with the relief of that drought-baked crocodile for rain. Still I find it incredible that it was in my lifetime that, wan and wasted, Rosa Parks had been expected to stand on a bus yawning with empty seats because she was black. But then, I reflected, perhaps in the way that it is only via wrong questions that we arrive at the right ones, maybe you can only get to real virtue by way of wrong. Without Caesar's wickedness, there would have been no Christ. '… and unto God, that which is God's.'

"The most insulting thing I have ever heard," Ulm continued, once he had shoved his way forcefully enough through the throng to join us, "is that nothing in God's universe happens by accident. Who could possibly pray to a God Who countenanced the Holocaust or the economic holocaust of today? Who allows children to die in agony or Who does not intervene to stop a princess from being beheaded for adultery? Who turned deaf ears to the Black Death, the pandemics of history, today's of AIDS? A Supreme Being capable of any, and so many more, of these things is not a figure of admiration, and the only way He can be turned into a loving God is by a semantic and intellectual jiggery-pokery – which may fool the jiggery-pokers, but no one else.

"Having said that, it would be rash, I think," said Ulm, "to think there is not sometimes great wisdom contained in Man's invocation of God's word. The ten Commandments, for their time, were a sensible and laudable, and laudably simple, code of tenets on which to found a society. But if you want proof that they were written by Man, and not by God, you need look only at the third."

"Commandment?" you asked.

"Yes," he replied.

"'Thou shalt not take the name of the Lord thy God in vain'?"

"Your years in the convent were not entirely wasted, then," I commented, trying to raise a laugh. I needed to get some heat on my shoulder. I even thought it might need a massage. A chubby woman, overladen with spewing shopping-bags, wheezed huffily as she glowered at me. I don't think I'd done anything to upset her. I think I just was there.

"Think about it, Sophia," Ulm advised.

"It was *Sóphia*," you corrected him. "Like the Bulgarian capital, with the stress on the first syllable. Now it's Giselle."

"Her birth name," I told him. "She's left the convent. She's a nurse now. That way, I suppose, she gets to stay a 'sister'." Proving yet again that comedy is not my strongest suit!

Ulm absorbed this information without comment, before continuing. "Think about it," he said. "We may never be able to know who God is, or what He is – or She or It. But we do know whatever God is God is something, if not omnipotent, of quite enormous and incalculable power. And yet we give credence that this Supreme Being should crave the vainglorious sycophancy of a tinpot dictator, a Mussolini or a Mugabe, or of a film director. This is not only to debase God to man's level, but to a fairly base level even of Man. It is to disobey its own tenet. Because there could be no finer example of taking God's name in vain than to think God capable of such vainness.

"Anyone with any faith at all in a god knows God loves a joke. He has to. We are surely not suggesting that God is capable of laughing at us, whilst forbidding us to laugh at him. That is to equate God with some kind of Hell-fire-and-brimstone minister.

"No, those are not God's words. The Commandment is designed to remove God from the public domain, render Him something esoteric and difficult, endowed with a mystique it is the privilege of only a few to understand. Akin to making God omnipotent. Priests, in other words, invented that Commandment. And simply in order to wrest more power."

We struggled off the bus, up the hill home. An old fiddler screeched at the corner, busking for cents. It didn't help my mood. You ran me a bath, almost plonked me in it. You wanted to use the phone, were anxious when you found it to be out of order. I told you, the next day I would call and report it, get it fixed. Whilst I soaked, you made tea. You and Ulm were drinking yours when, the pain now subsided into a dull thud and wearing that towelling robe of mine, I returned to the sitting room.

As I sipped, I said to you, "I've got a question for you. A good one, I think."

"Okay," you said. There was a solicitousness in your voice which I suspected was that of the professional carer. But I was in so much pain, it had started to affect my hearing.

"Bertrand Russell was a great man," I said. "Both a good man and a *great* man. And an atheist."

"Many good and great men have been atheists," said Ulm.

"And women," you reminded him.

"He was once asked, Russell," I continued, "what he would say to God when he met Him in the next world. 'Simple,' Russell replied. 'I'd just ask Him why He gave me no conclusive proof of His existence.'

"And that too is a good question," I said. "An entirely reasonable and good question. So good, in fact, that it has kept many an atheist in his faith without need of further thought. I came to the conclusion, oh long before I met Arkona, that if God did provide such proof, then the mystery would be gone from God, that the mystery of God is elemental to God, and that therefore a God Who provided evidence of His existence could not *be* God.

"And so, whilst I continue to think Russell has a point, I tend to think it has the ring to it of your condemnation, Giselle, of logic: it is a synthetic truth and thus an incomplete one.

"A more difficult question for me is this: If there were a God, would there be a *need* of one?"

* * *

The waiting room was crowded. The hospital's authorities deemed it not yet hot enough to warrant the running costs of the air-conditioning. A cloying heat thus hazed around each being, and a languid stickiness clung to every surface.

To be sent to an Orphalese hospital for tests is, as you know, to be sentenced to a long wait. You know it and so do the patients. As they know there won't be chairs enough. Most had brought canvas stools or garden chairs or beach ones. One apparently aloof farmer brooded on a shooting-stick. He sported a huge handlebar moustache which he stroked incessantly. His manner was abrupt and fierce, but his conker brown eyes melted into the floor, as he squinted into a reverie which seemed to be the only analgesia available to him in what was clearly a furnace of pain.

Only when the bus was halfway there did it occur to me that I had forgotten my stool. I cursed myself royally. I'd put it by the door, precisely so I *could* not forget it. That little round stool, you know? The one whose cushioned grey top is now fading so badly? I almost never use it. Only really to reach that chicken-shaped casserole dish on the top shelf. Latterly my back has been hurting too much for me even to think about fetching that dish down. Not that I mind that much. If truth were told, casseroles, they're one of those things which I think I should like much more than I actually do.

The lone receptionist was a podgy woman in her forties, whose jet-black hair was cut bureaucratically short. I'm sure you know her. Her complexion was sallow, and her humour shallow. Oh, there was wit, even joy, in her eyes, but wit, joy and eyes seemed all to be drowning in the torrent of vicarious pain and confusion with which she was for ten hours a day confronted.

Alone she battled with constantly jingling phones, with the jangling anxiousness of the newly arrived, with the jingling-jangling frustrations of those who had been imprisoned there for hours more than they had feared. She dealt with the self-impor-tance of the doctors and the harriedness of the nurses, with the distress of the patients and the terror of those close to them. And mostly she did all that with a clipped courtesy which I'm sure she considers 'professional'. But sometimes the enamel chipped. And then she'd quit her post, flee into the open air and puff frantically on a small cheroot until that 'professional' equipoise had been resuscitated.

I was lucky. I found a chair. It was similar to a kitchen chair: chrome structure, cushions of black plastic. That of the seat had been slashed, leaving a scar which continued on into the yellow foam rubber. So old was the wound that now the exposed rubber had turned almost black, and had cauterised into terminal crumbliness.

The receptionist had given me a small ticket printed with the number '187'. When I arrived, the patient with number '24' was being seen. Several hours had already passed. They'd progressed to the patient with '62' on his ticket.

I had my eyes closed. It was just easier that way. Around me I could hear the constant shuffle of boredom: the pages of magazines being flicked – angry flicks sometimes, sometimes resigned flicks, flicks of tedium, exasperation, *des*peration and despond. I could hear the tap-dancing of sedentary feet on the linoleum floor, the bickering of children, the sighs, the tuts, the incessant shuffling of bottoms, the pacing and the yawning, the vacuous chatter to fill a silence ... the dread of silence ... the dread silence ... the silent dread ... the unspoken terror.

"Lakshmi!" exclaimed a surprised voice I knew so well.

"Giselle!" I exclaimed back, and rose that I might embrace you, and be embraced by you.

"What are you doing here?" you asked.

"Waiting," I replied. "Isn't that what everyone does here?"

"You know what I mean."

"Certain suspects, as the police would say, need to be eliminated from inquiries," I told you.

"You could have let me know," you complained. "I could have ... you know ... maybe done something to reduce the wait."

"I'm fine waiting, Giselle," I said, lying through my teeth. I wanted the truth to be that I didn't want to worry you. But the real truth is, I fear, that I didn't want to worry myself. If I'd let you know I was going for tests that would have been an acknowledgement to myself that there was something to worry about. I didn't want there to be anything to worry about. "I'm fine," I repeated. "Really."

"Right!" you replied and snorted. "What number are you?" I showed you my ticket. During the wait, I'd rolled it into a cylinder, then wiggled that cylinder back and forth, like a paper worry-bead. The number consequently could not now easily be read. When you eventually deciphered it, you said, "God, you'll be here for hours yet. I'm due lunch in a quarter-of-an-hour or so. We'll have a chat then. A real chat. You should have let me know," you repeated, a geyser of care and caring.

I was feeling awkward now. I felt that our conversation was a sonic boom over the still of a prairies' night, felt as if your sympathy looked ridiculous on me – mutton dressed as lamb –, that there were children there whom the sympathy would fit so much more elegantly.

Being savvy to hospital waiting, I had brought a packed lunch with me. You'd noticed that when you'd first seen me, and then – clearly – had promptly forgotten it. You therefore (but very sweetly) bought two sandwiches at the canteen, one for me, and two brown plastic cups of very strong, very bitter coffee sweetened liberally by the saccharine you remembered I prefer to sugar.

Outside the Casualty Department, there is that hemisphere of green, bordered by cypress trees. This seems to be the hospital's contribution both to the general concept of ecology and to the provision of the 'good view' which so many medical therapists now consider a boon to recovery. A few paths zigzag inside the hemisphere, a couple of uninspired flower-beds break the green monotony, a bench here and there is supposed to persuade us the 'park' is 'user-friendly'.

I'm probably being unfair but the overwhelming impression I'm left with by the 'park' is that the hospital's contribution to environment and beauty is desultory at best, and probably begrudging. Even the flowers seem to agree. And so, rather than glorying in their colours, they seem coy in them, embarrassed and self-conscious – like a tubby Saxon sausaged into a flamenco dress.

"I have a lover," you told me, almost as soon as we had sat down. You had led me to a bench in the shade of one of the cypresses. The midday sun was beginning to swelter, and most of those lunching were doing so indoors. There was a still surrounding us, as if the world were holding its breath. Even the smells seemed to have sidled off for siesta. The only things with energy were the noises: the buzz of insects, and the drone of the lunchtime traffic jam, its horns, its klaxons and its revving up engines.

"I didn't realise how incomplete I was feeling," you said. "So many things I didn't realise. I didn't realise how many smells there were on one body. Completely different smells. I didn't realise how many there were on mine! I didn't realise that bodies smelled so different when they are ... let's say ... passionate, nor when they are sleeping.

"And I didn't know, Lakshmi, it was possible to feel so many feelings at the same time – so many of them contradictory feelings. That I could at the same time feel so much attraction and so much revulsion, that pain and pleasure are not opposites but complements to each other. And, know what?, that had a wider dynamic, Lakshmi. Really. It also helped me realise that all the other times I'd had these apparently contradictory feelings running round in my head, that was alright too.

"I remember, for instance, when my father died, that evening there was such a lovely sunset. It was glorious. Those flying-saucer-like clouds tinged with all the deep, deep colours, you know, of purple and orange and mauve. A painter's orgy of colour. It was magnificent. But for years I never told anyone about it, because I felt that my noticing that sunset must mean my mourning for my father had to have been somehow deficient. Their neighbour, Mother's and Dad's, made us a stew. It was delicious. That deliciousness too I never dared to talk about.

"But I see now, we are capable, us humans, of feeling a jumble of different things at the same time. In fact, maybe that's *all* we do. We never feel an emotion in isolation. I see now that because I was broken-hearted about my father's death, that doesn't stop me from being able to enjoy other things in life. Nor does it mean, because I *am* able to enjoy those things, that I mourn my father less. I am right, Lakshmi, aren't I?"

"You don't need to ask me that," I replied. "Your answer is in the singing of your voice."

You blushed lightly. It was a touching sight. "When I say 'lover'," you continued, "I suppose what I should say, what would be more truthful to say, I really mean 'bedfellow'. I don't love him. Not yet, anyway. Well, not in the way that I imagine loving someone feels like. But I do love the feelings I have around him. I do love feeling him – physically, I mean – and being felt by him. I do love the welter of emotional feelings too. Most of all, though, Lakshmi, I *love* the principal feeling I have when I'm one with him: I love the feeling of being whole."

"It's not a new thought," I said, "how similar in sound and fact are 'whole' and 'holy', but it's always apposite."

"I *do* feel holy, Lakshmi. Wholer and holier than I ever did either as a nun. Or as a virgin. And you are right – or Ulm was right – my head's spinning so much, I'm really no longer sure who said what when … I'm not sure, truth to tell, about *anything*: There is so much mystery involved in it, in sex, there is so much that is sacred in it, a whole continent opens up which needs to be explored.

"There is as much mystery in sex as there is in music, as much is stirred up as by a great piece of abstract sculpture. More. It is a language of infinite wonder where words are as meaningless as bird-song, and quite as mellifluous.

"He's Jewish, Lakshmi," you continued, without even breaking stride. "Which is probably another of God's little jokes. His name's Ezekiel." And then you got serious. "He's also an addict. Oh, he's not using drugs at the moment. He's 'in recovery,' as he calls it. But, he says, still an addict. 'Once an addict, always an addict,' he says."

"Does that worry you?"

"Do you think it should?" you asked.

"Now, that is not a right question," I replied, with a smile, I'm afraid, that was forced.

"No," you agreed, "it's not. Does it worry me? Well, actually no. Actually not at all. In fact, if anything, it was *that* which worried me. Initially at least. That I *wasn't* worried, I mean. I felt I should be. But then I felt, 'Know what, Giselle? You worry too much.' I mean, we're always being told, aren't we – I mean, time and again – that we can only live for today? That yesterday is history and tomorrow is a mystery, all that? That all we have is the now?"

"That we should 'live in the day'?" I asked.

"Yes."

"You don't think it's possible, do you, that they've got the days mixed up?" I asked. I drank the dregs of the coffee. It was surprisingly good. The noontide congestion was now easing. The drone had gone of jam, there were less impatient horns being blared, less engines being revved. Instead there was the almost aquatic sjoosh of flow.

"Maybe I should check on how the queue's doing," I said. I brushed the sandwich crumbs from my lap, passed the empty plastic cup to you. "Thank you for lunch. Do you think you could get rid of that for me?"

"I have to get back as well. Could I see you home this evening?"

"Won't Ezekiel be expecting you?"

"Isn't it good for us sometimes to wait?"

We kissed and parted.

* * *

The department had been closed for over an hour when eventually I was seen. I think it is remarkable that the staff, unpaid for this overtime, still do it. I hear what you say: that unless they did, they would never keep pace. But I still find it remarkable.

I know you used your influence to ensure that I was seen that evening. I'm grateful to you for that. That doesn't sound very grateful, but I am. I know that those who arrived later than me were told to return the next day. When the whole shebang starts all over again. It's not that those not seen that day start at the head of the next day's queue. No. Tomorrow, the podgy receptionist will apply the same rules as she did today – and on every other day since she'd worked there: first come, first served. I heard many of those not seen today decide to stay the night. The receptionist did nothing to evict them. Eviction was not her job. Her job was to check patients in, not out.

We had a good moan together. And the moans we had, they were good moans too – some of them even bona fide ones; all of them ones which kept us occupied throughout the bus-trip home, on that same shiny bus. And through the dusty walk along my street, a street which seems to get longer each day. I don't need tests to tell me what's wrong. Physically I know what's wrong with me. I have since the pain in my shoulder started becoming stubborn. It's what's emotionally wrong with me that I find harder to fathom.

Why can I not yet tell you that I know what's wrong with me? Why can I not confide in you how scared, how *terrified* I am? Oh, not of death. I'm not scared of death. In fact, I'm surprised that so many people my age are. But – God knows – I'm scared of dying. I am so scared of dying that I'm past the point where any reassurance could reach me. There is only terror. And I would say to you – I would say to *anyone* – it's alright to be terrified, it's natural, but let the terror out, talk about the terror to someone. It'll take the sting out of it, it'll make it copable with. And I hear my own advice. And I know how sound it is. And still I cannot take it.

We both had showers, washed away some of the day's dust, cooled down some of the evening's lingering heat. You were squeezing lemons in the kitchen.

"Days mixed up?" you asked.

"Sorry?" I said. I'd sat down at the kitchen table. I was allowing the lemons to do their worst with my saliva ducts. There are elements of powerlessness that I rather enjoy – and that a cut lemon inevitably makes you salivate is one.

"At the end of lunch, you said that when we talk of 'living in today' we get the day mixed up. I've been wondering all afternoon what you meant."

"I fear it is a problem with the world we live in today that we do exactly that: we live in today," I said. "Well, maybe not in it, but certainly *for* it. Our age is one, Giselle – you hinted at it yourself –, of instant gratification. Which makes it the age of the baby. What we are told is a 'sophisticated' economy, in other words, is based on nothing more profound or altruistic than a baby's cravings!

"Surely, the day we must live in is not today, but tomorrow," I suggested. You passed me the citron pressé you had made. "Do you think this might taste better with a little white rum?" I asked.

"Why not?" you said.

We added the rum, took our drinks out onto the balcony. The sun was starting to think about setting. But the heat coming up from the cobbles had not yet heard it.

"Arkona said, 'Tomorrow whistles the tune composed by today.' But it's more than that, I think," I said. "We all know from the cliché that the man who eats his cockerel today eats but once. But even more foolhardy is the man who eats that cockerel believing that tomorrow it will be God Who somehow fertilises his hens. Miraculously or otherwise. That man, in my opinion, is being crass – maybe even to the point of blasphemy. Such is not faith, but idiocy. And there's part of the cockerel eater which knows that. And the part that knows it ruins even the meal for the part that refuses to acknowledge it.

"If we are going to live contentedly today, Giselle, we must be at peace with today. For us to be at peace with today it is a requirement that we are at peace with at least two other things: yesterday and tomorrow." You had your eyes closed, were absent-mindedly running your fingers through your hair as the sun's rays tangoed on its wetness.

"Conscience is thought of as a killjoy," I continued. "But it's really not. *Really* not. It's a well-kept secret, but, tended well, conscience is actually the secret passage to great joy. Because what conscience does, eventually it allows you to become yourself. In fact, it is not in my view possible *to* become yourself without having nurtured your conscience. And with that nurture comes the realisation that, like pain, it is not an enemy but an ally."

I took a sip of my drink. Not only was it delicious, but it hit a much needed spot. "The *nurture* of conscience, Giselle, consists of only one thing, but that one thing is, I think, an absolute requirement – that your conscience becomes exactly that: *your* conscience.

"Historically we have allowed our conscience to be decided by those of others, or by the insistence of others – particularly others in our family or in the Church. This is just as much an invasion as that of a country occupied by foreign troops. And in the same way as you would with such troops, the best way of dealing with them is to oust them as soon as possible.

"Shame is exactly such an invasive force. Those who try to shame us try to tell us shame is synonymous with guilt. But shame and guilt are as similar as arsenic and old lace. They are associated together in our brains, but one is toxic, and the other can be both useful and attractive. Guilt, properly applied, is a tool which can help us – in fact, one of conscience's finest.

"Shame, on the other hand, would have us being 'shame-faced' about, I don't know, farting, say (even when we're alone), or masturbating ..."

"God, Lakshmi ... I've never ... " This time I had no need to see your blush. I could hear it in your stammer.

"Well, if you ever do, is all I'm saying, ask yourself whether there is any reason to feel guilty about it. If not, then you have no reason to feel shame. Shame is what we contract from the neuroses of others. A part of our shame we inherit from our parents or our schoolteachers; another part, inevitably, is a compote of the neuroses of society as a whole, which that society insists become our own. And which we allow to become our own.

"Guilt, on the other hand, is an entirely different matter. Guilt helps us to move forward. Our guilt for an offence yesterday does not directly make our today any better, but it will improve our tomorrow – and knowledge that our tomorrow will be better, already does (even if only indirectly) improve our today. Enough pain about yesterday will stop us from repeating the guilt-inducing act today. And that will directly and positively improve our tomorrow, because if we don't commit the same offence today, tomorrow we *won't* feel guilty about it. And we know that."

"Obviously," you said.

"Obviously, as you say," I said. "I've got news for you, Giselle, *most* of what we need to know is obvious. Oscar Wilde once commented that there is nothing less common than common sense.

Ulm was talking about mankind's commitment to survive. A big step in that commitment would be the greater application of common sense."

"More citron pressé?" you asked, waving the rum bottle.

"Very many more of these citrus drinks, I'll be quite squiffy," I said.

"Doctor's orders," you quipped back. "Nurse's orders, anyway." And you poured a jigger of the drink, with considerably more rum than citron! I took another slug. It was easing the pain in my shoulder far more effectively than any of the drugs I had been taking.

"There's more to guilt, Lakshmi, than that," you commented.

"Oh, of course there is," I agreed. "If yesterday I did something which has caused me to feel guilty today I also need to consider the appropriateness of, for example, reparation – another way in which I make my tomorrow a better place. And if yesterday I have been wronged, I might think about forgiveness. Not so that the tomorrow can be better for the person who has wronged me, but so that mine can.

"That's all dealing with yesterday, Giselle. What, you may very reasonably ask, about the much trumpeted today? *Today*, I also need to feel that I am doing everything possible to make tomorrow a better place. Even those with terminal illnesses need to feel that." It just slipped out. It wasn't a conscious decision; not even, I think, a Freudian slip, just my mouth racing ahead of my brain. You darted a look at me. And then pretended you hadn't. And I pretended I hadn't noticed.

"If I take my medicine tonight," I said, leaping in to cover even the hint of a pause, "I will have done all in my power to ensure that tomorrow I feel better. At least I won't feel worse. And I won't feel worse because I can, in all conscience, tell myself, when tomorrow arrives, that I did do everything possible to improve what is now my today. My tomorrow has to be better, if for no other reason, than for a lack of self-recrimination. It doesn't matter if I die tonight. Why should that matter?

"If you doubt any of this, ask yourself this one question: 'Wouldn't it have been nice if we had been born into a planet where rather more thought *had* been devoted to our tomorrow?' And the world into which I was born, Giselle, had considerably more concern about the future – albeit, often misguided concern – than the world into which you were born. And that world had considerably more than today's.

"You're sleeping with a junkie. 'Living in today', as it is chosen to be interpreted by vested interest today, is the axiom not of the wise man but *of* the junkie. And not a junkie, as you put it, 'in recovery', but one still active and stoned.

"To live in today can never be to ignore either yesterday or tomorrow. Today has to deal with them as thoroughly as it can so that both impinge as little as possible on it. Today is like a dish of strawberries topped with sugar and cream. All three elements exist in their own right. But their sum is greater than their parts, and they complement one another by counterpointing the other: the tart with the sweet, the solid with the liquid, the granular with the smooth. When we eat strawberries, don't we always make sure that there is still enough sugar left to eat with the last strawberry, enough cream to go on top?

"If today's politicians are right – and those economists whose views are allowed common currency – and the so-called 'third way', the way of globalisation, is the only way forward, we are doomed.

"Globalisation, as I've already said, is the economics of the crib. Would you ask a toddler to guide you through a minefield? We don't have one minefield in the world today, we have minefields which stretch the length of continents. We need not only adults to guide us, but extremely wise adults, and ones who don't pay lip service to common sense, but actually apply it.

"Of course, it is an important element in each of us, the famous child within. But we don't ask the advice of that child, if we are wise, when thinking about the house we might buy, or the career move we might make. When we make our big decisions, we need to be the most grown-up us we can be. 'When I was a child, I thought as a child ...' I'm sure you remember. 'But now I am a man ...'

"What distinguishes the adult from the child? Emotionally, I mean? Intellectually? Surely, it has to be the concern we demonstrate for others. I mean, isn't that it?

"When in the history of humanity have selfishness, self-centredness, self-seeking been lionised in the way they are today?

"Your friend, Ezekiel again, à propos of him, I know of an alcoholic, told by his doctor that if he continued to drink in the way he had been, he would be killed by liquor in six months. He went straight from the surgery to the bar, and told his cronies there that his doctor had given him six months to live. And used the 'fact' of his imminent demise as a pretext to drink even more.

"Isn't that entirely analogous to what the world today is doing to itself? It is seeking as a cure for its sickness the very thing that is making it sick."

"If not the world, then the Holy Ghost?" you suggested.

"As you say," I said.

"Do you think the Holy Ghost has any kind of spiritual dimension today?"

"Isn't that exactly the God you were talking about, the God of a godless world?"

"But He's as godless *as* the world."

"No, His godliness is hiding. The world has become secular, because people misunderstand God. They have in many instances been betrayed by the ministers of God – in *so* many instances –, that they think it is God who has betrayed them. They need to reclaim God. They need, as Arkona urged, to define their own God – or come to terms with *their own* lack of definition about God.

"Castigated about the popularity of the music used by the Salvation Army, its founder famously remarked: 'Why should the devil have all the best tunes?' Why should those who appear to want to destroy the world adopt God as their own? Why do those of us who want a future for this planet allow them to? Why, because so much of the established Church (in its plurality) gives sanction and credence to these vandals, do we allow the Church to confiscate from us what is our birthright, the ownership of God?

"Are you staying the night?"

"I'd like to," you said. Bless you. I made no comment. But I was happier than you could imagine. "We'll stop our cogitation now, and concentrate on these excellent drinks. But in your drunken stupor later," I said, "think why it is the first Commandment *is* the first Commandment."

"Cheers," you said.

"Your very good health," I returned.

"And yours," you fired back, with undisguised significance. We clinked glasses.

* * *

The young sleep so soundly. It's yet something else the old envy in you: we the old, I mean. You are no exception. I feared when the phone went, it would wake you. I suppose, looking back on it now, it might have been better if it had.

I knew what the phone call was about, of course: the results of the tests. I didn't really need them. They merely confirmed what my body had already told me.

The oncologist was very kind. She told me about the operation I needed immediately, to relieve some pressure on my spine. Without which, she told me, it could snap at any moment and leave me paralysed from the waist down. She described to me carefully and – no pun intended – painstakingly the likely consequences of the radiotherapy on which, after the operation, they will embark. There was a smile in her voice which was one that seems to be common to all the medical staff with whom I have now come in contact: the nurses, radiologists, the supervisors of endless probes and scans – and bleeps and whirrs and cylinders and needles.

The window of my bedroom faces, as you know, almost exactly due East. Through it I am used to seeing a steep hill of coarse grass and crab grass which, decades previously, an ambitious farmer had tried to terrace, before being beaten by the ruggedness of the terrain.

Beyond this hill is the sea, and the hill drops away sufficiently at one point for me to be able to see a sliver of that sea, usually glinting beneath a careless sun. The sun that each morning I watch rise, and whose rise I never tire of watching. I've watched that rise for over twenty years. Never in that time have I watched it rise the same way twice. There's been the odd day when the cloud has been such, the indication of dawn was only an intimation of it; on all the rest, the bacchanal there was of hue and resonance and texture rarely failed both to woo and to wow me. Increasingly, now that my sight is weakening, I have to *feel* that wooing and that wowing. But feel them I do – through the thousand natural shocks that flesh is heir to: the warmth on my cheek of its rays, the song of the birds, the intensity of the rainbow *my* side of my eyes. Still the magentas are of petunias of the plushest velvet, the orange of marigolds and liquid fire, the yellows of daffodils, feathered like canaries. And still each morning I gaze at it and glory in it.

That morning was no exception. I'd risen to brew the coffee, and had taken the pot back with me to the bedroom – plus an extra mug for you. As I do each day I stirred that sunrise into my coffee, and drank them down together. Each day consequently, and that day too, is a day which starts blissfully. Even with a pain in the neck.

The sun had just crept above the copse of palm trees in the distance. You wandered in, rubbing the sleep from your eyes.

"I smelt coffee," you said.

"Help yourself," I told you.

You pounced on the pot rather as a starving leopard seizes on a wounded zebra. "Did I hear the phone?" you asked.

"Must have been the neighbours'," I replied, hating myself for lying, hating the cowardice in me that was causing me to lie. You held that blue mug in both hands, I remember, and drank the first swallow with your eyes closed, apparently basking in the coffee's slide down your throat. When you opened your eyes, you looked for a long time silently at the view. I joined you in your gazing.

Without any further preamble, suddenly you incanted, "'I am the Lord, thy God. Thou shalt have no other gods before me.'" You sat on the edge of the bed, and angled yourself so that you looked away from the view. It was almost as if that way you could listen more intensely. But your eyes were still sticky with slumber. "What you said, Lakshmi, the other day, about the Judaeo-Christian God recognising the pantheon inside all of us, that's what you meant, isn't it?"

"Yes," I replied.

"'… no other gods *before* me'?"

"Quite," I said.

"It's the Three in One, isn't it," you suggested, "and the One in Three? The Lord, our God, I should probably say? The Lord our God of the Commandment? I've been thinking about it all night. I think, maybe, I'm beginning to understand that."

I remembered the vision of you sleeping comatosely and – don't be angry with me, Giselle – smiled at myself that you should have considered that 'thinking all night'. "The Lord thy God or the King of kings," I intoned.

"Yes," you said, for want of anything else to say.

"Just to detour for a moment, you're alright, are you, with those phrases? You find nothing … awkward about them? Objectionable? The expression, I mean, 'the Lord, thy God'? 'The King of kings'?"

"I obviously should," you replied.

"I do. That doesn't mean you have to," I reminded you.

"Go on," you said. You waved the coffee pot at me, inviting me to a second cup. When I declined, you topped yourself up.

"Both humanise God," I suggested. "Both, as Arkona put it, 'seek to put a face on the wind'."

"Isn't that part of the metaphor you were talking about?"

"Of course," I said. "But it does leave the door wide open for abuse. It also, of course, seeks to validate kings."

"It does?" you asked, gazing ever more deeply into the view.

Your eyebrows furrowed into the light ridge you have when you are concentrating. It exposes your intelligence more nakedly than an x-ray.

"If kings kowtow, at least publicly, to the King of kings," I said, "if they convince us they believe in His sovereignty and acknowledge obedience to His whim, are not those kings trying to tell us non-kings (us who are not kings) that we owe the same kind of allegiance to them, our *earthly* kings, the kings of commoners? Isn't it comparable to Augustus building a statue to Julius Caesar, setting such in the Roman pantheon, then claiming to be the stepson of a god? Does not the nomenclature 'the Lord' give authority to *feudal* lords?

"And if any of this is the case, how can the Church possibly claim that it is not stealing from God and rendering that which should be God's unto Caesar? How is this not Faust, but a Faust applauded by our spiritual mentors? How is this not Esau – selling our birthright, which is our conscience, our integrity, our godliness as manifested in the Son, for a mess of potage, which is blind allegiance to a king or a country – or even a Faith?

"A Faith which demands blind allegiance cannot be divine. It has to be contrived and it has to serve the interest, not of God, but of the contrivers.

"Hence, for example, patriotism. Patriotism is not only the last vestige of the scoundrel, it is the first arrow in the quiver of the unprincipled. When religion countenances in this way the status quo, you just know it has lost touch with God the Father. It is not even the Holy Ghost, but a version of the Holy Ghost being distorted by those claiming to serve Him."

"I think," you said, "there may be those who disagree."

"Of course. Who even violently disagree. But far more try to tell themselves either that it is irrelevant, or that it is irrelevant to *them*. We don't care about the moral calibre of our governance, so much as its physical effects on us. We're brought up to believe that we will never understand the 'wider picture' and that we should leave such consideration to our 'wisers and betters'.

"So many of us, we really don't like taking responsibility for ourselves. We're instructed from infancy not to do so. Oh, we're told we're responsible for paying our bills, that yes. But we are not responsible for the ethical fabric of our economy. The scapegoat god Ulm was talking about, for a lot of us, has become the scapegoat government or the scapegoat economic climate ... or the scapegoat anything else. "

"Yes, Lakshmi," you said, with a rancour that tasted very sharp in the early morning sunlight. "And there are those too who accuse the starving of not taking responsibility for themselves, who consider AIDS orphans to have brought their woes on themselves or who tut that South American street children don't go to school."

"Oh, governments don't want us to take responsibility for ourselves," I returned quickly. I was hurt by what seemed to be your rebuke, but I didn't want to dwell on it. I realised I too tend to address most sharply those people with whom I disagree only on detail. "Nor does the Church, or industry. They pay lip-service to it, but do nothing in practice. And, of course it's grotesque when the grotesquely deprived are blamed for their fate. But that too is about control.

"We need to ask ourselves, I think, how sincere is the commitment government has to eradicating that obscene deprivation, and how much it suits its purposes to keep present the awful threat to us all, such deprivation represents.

"Governments talk about us taking responsibility for ourselves as though that were something innate, and a failure to do so is akin to failing to eat when we are hungry. It isn't. And if it is, it is an instinct which a lot of us have lost. Myself included. If governments were really serious about our taking such responsibility, why hasn't that skill been added – and as a priority – to the school curriculum?"

"Okay, Lakshmi, diversion over."

"You intimated, Giselle, that you wanted to talk about the first Commandment. This is *it*: the first Commandment. It's fundamental. We can never satisfy that Commandment in a global, or in a universal, way because there is the element – God, if you like, the Son – which has to be particular to us all.

"But in a nutshell, and insofar as we *can* apply it universally, it is really just another way, the first Commandment, of recognising that element particular to us all: It is a synonym for Polonius's famous dictum: 'Unto thine own self be true'. It is an exhortation to find in you your own God – God the Son – and the courage to obey only the dictates of God-the-Son's Father, Who is, of course, God the Father. In other words, to find your soul, and to remain truthful to it." I hesitated before I added, "With which there is only one problem."

"And that is?" you asked.

"I think Hitler *was* true to himself," I admitted. "I think Narcissus was and Henry Ford. You can, in other words, be true too to a warped soul. Indeed, those whom we know about with warped souls seem, to a man, to be true to them. And what you do about that, I really do not know. But then, any theory I might have stumbled across which did have all the answers would *really* worry me.

"Arkona was so right when he urged us to look for the question and not the answer.

"Do you not think, if Communism and Capitalism had devoted the time to questions that they both devoted to statements, that the world today might not now be *extricating* itself from some of its problems? Instead of plunging blindly forward in a whirlwind of further statements, creating ever more problems?

"If both '-isms', in other words, rather than on insisting that they were right, had expended that energy on *asking* themselves *whether* they were? Asking themselves, even more importantly, where they were *wrong*? Even if they'd expended *half* that energy? If, instead of criticising their neighbour's back-yard, they had cleaned up their own?

"Do you think *today* we might provide some tangible future, rather than by always bragging about the breadth of our knowledge, by seeking to define the infinite of our ignorance?

"Where are any questions today? All those questions which wisdom trawls? Which it has to trawl? How often do we even *hear* questions?

"And how often statements?

"The West used to deride, and with some justification, those dictatorial nations with 'Democratic' in their names. But which of those deriders is itself truly democratic?

"The last thing politicians want is for more people to join in the political debate. They want more people to vote, certainly. It's becoming derisory, the size of the turnout. And thus their claim of a 'mandate'. Governments fear disenchantment with the polling booth will lead the electorate to find other ways to take 'responsibility for themselves' – through civil disobedience, for instance, even violent confrontation. Or even just through a truculent discontentedness.

"And governments are right to fear it. Violence is latent on the streets of so many Western cities. What government neglects to mention, of course, is that such violence is one which has been learnt from government – from both it and from its economic strategists. If you plant acorns, you get oaks. And this is, yes, Giselle, all part of the first Commandment. It is all about remaining true to yourself.

"How democratic is the Church, for that matter? How much say does the member of a Catholic congregation have in the choice of Pope? How many Jews choose the Chief Rabbi? Muslims their Ayatollahs?

"By defining God, the Church robs from God that which is God's and renders it, shamelessly, unto Caesar. The Church has clashed with the state only when one has sought to attack the vested interest of the other. The interest of both should be Man. But the interests of both are the subjugation, not the liberation, of Man. And as such both transgress more mightily against the first Commandment even than those whose contempt is such they claim to spit on God."

"You're quite scary, Lakshmi," you said, "when you get angry."

"It is desecration," I said, hearing your words, but not *really* hearing them. "It is far more blasphemous than a poem about the fantasy of an affair Jesus might have had with a centurion. It is a blasphemy against the Holy Spirit which we all contain, and against the Holy Ghost, which is that spirit freed to care for the world.

"Blasphemy is the deliberate misinterpretation of God. If someone interprets God for you, they *have* to be misinterpreting God. Because they are not you and because, by definition, only you can."

"I'm going to make some more coffee. Shall I also make breakfast?" you asked. I think you expected me to say that *I* would.

Instead I said, "How lovely. Fresh rolls you can get from the corner shop. Not the so-called baker's. The corner shop before it."

"Right."

"But you want to get home, no?"

"No, Lakshmi," you said, trying – I think – to convince yourself. "No, really. There is a part of my brain I've underused. I don't know which part precisely. All of it, probably. But I can feel the cogs churning. It's actually quite uncomfortable. But," you added assuming a funny voice I've never heard you use before, "them cogs, they do need to churn."

"We've nine Commandments left to go," I warned you.

"Eight."

"Eight?"

"The third I think we've already dealt with."

"And the second, that of making no graven images, I had always thought was an underscoring of what we have already talked about: That by trying to define God, you push God further away. God, in the Sistine Chapel, was far more in evidence, far more vibrant in Michelangelo's talent than in His depiction on the ceiling."

"I'll get dressed, get the rolls," you said. "Then we need to go shopping, Lakshmi. I don't want you carrying heavy stuff around, not with your shoulder like that."

"It's nothing, Giselle," I told you. "Really. Don't make a fuss."
But you'd already walked out of the room.

* * *

It was mid-morning. There was the usual bustle thronging the streets of Orphalese. It seems to reach its peak at about this time – when the sun's heat is still warmth and empowering, before it becomes torpor and debilitating.

It amazes me that carts still trundle the narrow streets of our tiny wall-defined town. I both love and hate the way their metal rimmed wheels clatter on the cobbles. In a gritty kind of syncopation, the off-key steel drums of torrential rain trampolining on sheets of corrugated iron. The noise grates, but I love the idea that it still pervades.

As I love the hawkers yelling and the horns hooting, even the phones trilling tinnily through open windows. I love the smell of lamb sizzling on those outside spits, and of the peanuts as they're dipped into that bubbling jasmine-smelling honey. These smells mix with the fumes of the thundering motorbikes, which hurtle their murderous, *suicidal* slaloms through swathes of cars and buses, pedestrians and other bikes. No anthill is more intricate in the patterns it weaves, nor in the myriad of different moves that form the choreography of this human stream. And no representation of the difficulty caused by the old living alongside the new is more trenchant than the recognition that so many of today's traffic jams are caused by yesterday's architecture.

The dress too of those around us, that reflected many of the dichotomies of Orphalese, much of its dilemma. Some of the shoppers held out neon tentacles to the glitz of the twenty-first century, but some held out a desperate withering limb to its past. As the traffic was to its architecture, so in dress and customs Occidentalism is swamping our ancient culture. And yet those roots still stubbornly refuse to wither.

You led me through the throng deftly and, apparently, effortlessly. We both agreed it would be nice to combine shopping with a cake at Buri's and a glass of citron pressé.

In looks, the waiter was almost a caricature barber: ovular face with sleaked hair parted in the centre and a moustache the ends of which were waxed. A hand was constantly hovering around his mouth as if just to suppress a burp or disguise one. Having taken our order, he disappeared into Buri's patisseried interior. We both sighed from relief at sitting down, taking the weight off our feet, and the weight of the shopping off our shoulders – yours, I will cheerfully concede, in particular. We smiled at one another, allowed ourselves to feel the kiss of the sun.

I was amazed you didn't know what tsifalla was, staggered that you had never tried one. "Tsifalla," I explained, "is an Orphalese sort of cake. You've probably got something similar in Syracuse. It's made with ginger mixed with chopped almonds and spices, covered in a very dark, very thick chocolate. They're tiny, Giselle. They look like a large sweet. But don't be fooled, they are enormously filling." And then I saw her. "Saskja!" I exclaimed.

You'll remember what happened then. To begin with, the teenager pretended she hadn't heard. But when I hailed her again she looked furtive and, eggshelled with guilt, rushed over to our table. "Please don't tell, Lakshmi," she gasped. "It's Italian." Her words torrented from her in such a garble they were in danger of tripping over each other. "It's Signora Bertorelli. She's awful. A cow. Only, please, Lakshmi, *please* – don't tell."

"Italian is a lovely language," I told her, probably as if I were imparting something new! "And Italy a lovely country, full of lovely food and wine. Full of lovely people."

"Except Milan," you added.

"Except Milan," I agreed.

"In that case," said Saskja, "Signora Bertorelli is like Prospero, '*absolute* Milan'."

"Oh, very good, Saskja," I said. And it was, don't you think?

Saskja accepted the compliment with a little bow of her head. And then continued, suddenly every inch the schoolgirl, "She's awful, Lakshmi. She picks on me non-stop. If your head's full of being picked on, how do you find space to learn anything?"

"Now, that is a good question," I said to you.

"Is that tsifalla?" Saskja asked, her eyes widened to Jersey cow proportions.

The barber-like waiter had brought our order and was placing it delicately in front of us. "The only thing better than hooky," I speculated, "is hooky with tsifalla, am I right?" Turning to the waiter I said, "You'd better bring us another." The waiter nodded that he had heard.

"I speak Italian," you told Saskja. "I'll teach you if you prefer." It was not your day for generous offers, Giselle! This one too, I think, you expected to be declined. And this one too was accepted.

Saskja said, "You know, I'd really like that. It's not that I don't want to learn," she continued. "It's just that with … Bertorelli I won't. Learn. Yes, great. *Great. Thank* you, Sóphia."

"It's Giselle now," you told her.

Over tsifalla and citron pressé your new situation was explained to the young woman. Well, most of it, anyway. No mention, I noticed, was made of Ezekiel or the role he was playing in your life. Is that a protection we have, do you think, of … I don't know … virginity or innocence or something? I remember wondering, when you were in the convent, why I was so taciturn about sex around you. I haven't gone any way to resolving that issue, beyond knowing it had a great deal more to do with me than you, and considerably more to do with secular qualms than spiritual ones.

Despite being only just a teenager, Saskja has, as we remarked later, the body almost of a woman. There is, you're right, still that podginess of a flesh that hasn't yet settled, maybe she has a tiny bit more to grow, bones and joints need to relax into their new situations, but her face – as you yourself later observed – is, for her years, remarkably clear and her hair remarkably silky. She is already such a pretty young woman, clearly en route to being a beautiful one. And it's not either that she's not conscious of her looks: there *is* a narcissism to her. But it doesn't seem to me that she wallows in it. Those big brown eyes of hers still burn with too much curiosity for that. I think, simply, she just doesn't have the time for that kind of vanity.

Indeed, if you remember, she didn't even have the time for tsifalla. She suddenly looked at her watch and realised, if she didn't get a move on, she'd be late for chemistry. She guzzled the drink and wolfed down the cake, eating the last of it as she hurtled down the street. She promised she'd come and visit us soon. It's not me she wants to see again, Giselle, but you. You made a big impression. I could see that. It's not Italian lessons she wants from you either, but lessons on life.

And you, my dear, with the younger woman, gave off an air of being almost matronly. And whilst you are a lot closer in years to Saskja than to me, when the teenager had left us, you felt – so it seemed to me – entitled to be admitted to the coven of elders. With which authority you commented, "Give her a year or two, she's going to break a few hearts."

"She'll break her own," I returned wryly. And sadly.

"Yes," you said. I don't think you were sure what I meant, but you felt that to admit that would see you expelled from the coven. And (for God only knows what reason) you wanted to stay. "Is there anything much to say about the fourth?" you asked, as if asking whether I'd like mushroom soup for lunch or tomato. I suppose I must have looked blank, because you quickly added, "Commandment, I should probably say. Is there much to say about the fourth *Commandment*?"

I'd left the money on the table to cover the bill. We were struggling to get our bags together. I was wondering, tell you the truth, whether we shouldn't get a taxi back. "Remind me what it is," I said.

"'Remember to keep holy the Sabbath Day': self-evidently, a Commandment we've let go of."

"Is it? Or is it yet another instance of our worshipping in our pantheon the cherub not the god? Is not the Sabbath Day kept holy by our going shopping on it? Is that not genuflecting, even *kowtowing*, in our veneration of Mammon? There really is nothing wrong with Mammon, but it is, I don't know, an Achilles (or someone) who has promoted itself to Zeus. Or who has been promoted to Zeus."

"You think?"

I looked sideways at you, with a 'what do *you* think' expression on my face. "What I think," I said, "is that we should get a taxi." You smiled skewiffly back at me, and then you saw a distant cab. You raised your arm and let out a whistle that would have shamed most doormen.

It was black, remember?, and collapsing. We couldn't get in the door behind the driver, had to go round the other side. If it had ever had suspension, it was something of distant memory. A Virgin Mary was blue-tacked to the top of the dashboard, a St Christopher medallion draped untidily around her neck. Pictures presumably of his two children in a frame of gilded plastic, the photos now so faded, only a father would be able to see his children in them.

We just plonked the shopping on our laps, as if we were both swaddling galumphing Tweedle-dees. The taxi jerked its unsteady progress, each hop accompanied by a click on the ancient meter.

Having got ourselves 'settled', I returned to the fourth Commandment, "There's nothing wrong with shopping on the Sabbath, except that it takes the shop assistants away from their families. Nor is there per se anything wrong with being advised once a week how to live your life. Even by people – priests, in other words – whose life experience is cloistered. What does matter is *why* you are doing these things.

"Those, in my opinion, who keep the Sabbath holy are those who use it to keep whole. Remember we talked in another context about the similarity between whole and holy. They keep themselves whole by devoting time to those things which make them whole. Themselves, their physical and emotional well-being, their beliefs and values, their families.

"The fourth Commandment, in my opinion, is an enjoinment both to reflect and relax. It is as holy a use of the Sabbath to get a massage as to attend a mass.

"There's certainly nothing wrong with washing your car on it. If that gives you pleasure. Maybe it could give you more pleasure if, whilst waxing, you were taking stock of the week that had just passed. And, as you vacuumed round the seats, wondering just how true you *had* been to yourself; asking yourself where in your life you could be more truthful. But if you don't want to do that, just washing it is fine. It's good exercise. And even that will serve to clear your mind of much of the week's debris.

"It seems to me a good use of the Sabbath to, I don't know, paint a portrait or paint the kitchen, to run a Marathon or run a stall at the local fête, to play badminton or play the banjo – or, best of all, play with the children. And to enjoy the return to one's own childhood which that can involve. Meditation's great, but so is mediation – in family squabbles, for example. Talking to one's children, what a great way of keeping the Sabbath holy. Listening to them, an even greater way. What greater way to keep yourself whole and them whole, the present whole and the future. You keep the Sabbath holy, as I say, if you use it to keep yourself whole."

The taxi made a final jolt, the full-stop at the end of a lot of semi-colons. I obviously tipped him too much as he emerged, his face mooning a cracked-lip grin, to crank open the back door for us. Shopping was distributed around cupboards, fridge and freezer. The heat was beginning to swelter. You made me sit at the kitchen table, poured us both a drink of ice-cold water. You asked me to continue.

"My problem with today's lack of Sabbath is that today we lack a special day. How do families become families without special days? We have allowed industrialists to build an economy which requires us to abandon special days – which is to demand the sacrifice of the future at the altar of the present," I said.

"The family days they have left us are all *commercial* days: Christmas and birthdays, in some countries Epiphany, Mother's day and, latterly, Valentine's day and Father's day. All excuses for those selfsame industrialists further to line their coffers, all pandering to the most base of instincts within us, all living off the terror we most of us have that our value as people is only equal to the value of the gift we tender.

"The propaganda machine which feeds that terror is colossal. Enormous. Billions are poured into that machine. Why? Because even more billions pour out of it. Our economy depends on it. In the same way that a brewer's profits depend on alcoholics. And that is an entirely appropriate analogy because that's what all this shopping is, a sickness. It emanates from a lack of self-worth, or of self-worthiness. The cloying dependence for others' approval which is the consequence of that. The unscrupulous way in which that is exploited by those with a vested interest to keep us sick.

"In the midst of which sickness, the spiritual side of love gets almost totally smothered. It is indeed a tribute to the strength of the spirit of love that it has not been completely vanquished.

"Historically, fathers have been considered the 'heads' of households: patriarchs; and mothers matriarchs. The patriarch, though, does not head a family but a fiefdom. And a matriarch does not rear children but clones." You poured some more water, passed it silently to me.

"We're now realising that very, very, *very* few delinquents are born. By far the biggest factor in the creation of a delinquent is not, actually, a childhood lack of love – it is the *perception* of the infant, rightly or wrongly, that he or she is not loved. And quite often the infant gets that perception because he is starved of time. Not this much-vaunted 'quality time': the ten minutes to read a story before bed, or the 'let's-bond' time, those are easy. It's the 'unquality' time, that's much more difficult: the time of just being one of a clan, if you like (each member of which is him- or herself and each one of which is encouraged to be so), whilst also belonging to something greater, not than the sum of its parts, but more than any one of them: the family. And this – albeit far too slowly – is being acknowledged."

I took a sip of the water. I was beginning to feel very hot. I thought it was the weather. "Yet we continue to witness politicians and business magnates throwing up despairing hands about the level of delinquency, whilst they confiscate from parents the time necessary to reduce the risk of it.

"If we continue to supply the pyromaniac with paraffin we cannot really be surprised at the instances of arson.

"Nor can we really complain if it is *our* house which is torched!

"The very institutions which rant at us about our lack of moral fibre, about our betrayal of the principles contained in the Ten Commandments (Commandments upon which our code of ethics is based and the morality supporting our jurisprudence), it is they who most flagrantly transgress them: the Church, the state, industry."

"You look tired," you said. "I'm so sorry. I should have noticed earlier. Even in the midst of all your indignation, Lakshmi, you look tired."

"You're right," I replied. I'd forgotten about my shoulder, but now the pain came swimming determinedly back, like a salmon about to spawn. "I think maybe I should lie down."

"Would you like me to massage that shoulder for you?"

"It just needs rest. Maybe an aspirin, though. For the pain."

"Aspirin for the soul. That's what we need, Lakshmi. What the whole world needs in fact."

"We have one," I said. "It's called talking."

* * *

The next time I saw you was in the hospital.

You'd come to see me before the operation, of course. For a visit. Grapes and gossip. Gentle talk about the flat and work, Ezekiel, talk about the lousy hospital food and of the party we'd have when I came out, reassuring talk that my surgeon was the best, the *very* best ... and no talk of pain or of illness or of death.

A wise friend of mine once told me that it is always the pain that keeps us apart. Us, the two halves of a relationship. It is not the things said which upset us, but the things unsaid. And it was those things then that I left unsaid which wounded me. More than that which I knew *you* had left unsaid. How much pain do we inflict on each other trying to save that person pain? Is that another of the great ironies of life?

I never told you I loved you. I find it hard to forgive myself for that. I could have died on the operating table. You know I love you, and I know you know I love you. But I have never told you. And that is a lack more in my life than it is in yours.

The first sight I remember which told me I was still on Earth was Ulm's toothless grin. Small wonder I opted almost immediately to return to coma! I remember after that a slurried montage of that grin and you, Saskja – I think –, of blue dresses and white aprons and white *coats*, and stethoscopes and drips and bleeps and sleeps and sleep, sheets, white sheets, and wooziness and fuzziness and white and blue and cleaners and lights and lights in my eyes and needles and waves of nausea and waves of sleepiness – sleepiness within the sleep, dreams of dreaming.

It was only shortly before my discharge that we returned again to the ten Commandments. I had to wear a constant neck-brace then, remember? It made it difficult to look around, discouraged me from changing focus from one person to another. Ulm had been sucking at my grapes. I am aware of the lack in his mouth of teeth – his incisorial incapacity, if you will – but the way he was sucking, and obliviously, at my grapes was, if I'm honest, beginning to irritate me. They were indeed grapes of wrath! Wrath inducing, anyway: the grapes that grate!

"'Honour thy father and mother'," you announced, even before you had finished closing the door. You carried more grapes – why grapes?, I've often asked myself – and a bunch of lilacs, their purple so dark almost as to be black, their texture sheening in the artificial light. You dragged over a chair, kissed me, and sat down. Then handed me the bouquet and the fruit, and continued, "I remember Arkona suggesting that should rather be 'Honour thy children'."

"I think," I corrected you, I hope mildly, "he wondered how different things might have been had that been the case. I don't think he would have disputed how important it is to honour those who have given you life and who have reared you. I can't answer for him, of course, but I would have thought such rather depended on what you mean by the word 'honour'. Venerate? No. Idolise? Most certainly not. But 'honour', yes, that's an appropriate feeling to have for people who have lavished that much care on you."

"Wasn't it to ensure that the elderly were looked after by their own family?" you asked. "That they weren't a drain on the community as a whole?"

Ulm remained contemplative and silent, sucking suckily on those damned grapes, as I replied, "Probably. At one level, anyway. I agree with Ulm that there are some inspired things contained within these Commandments, albeit sometimes fairly well buried within them. Some things *so* inspired, indeed, that I think they *are* God's work.

"At which level I think the fifth Commandment is an invocation to learn from history. Which would be splendid, but for one little thing: We are, as a species, so bad at it. God, Giselle, we're bad enough learning the lessons of our own past, let alone that of someone else. Apparently we each of us have to burn our own fingers on the fire. And most of us have to burn our fingers several times!"

Ulm stopped 'graping' for just long enough to add, "In which, for me, the oddest thing of all is that most of us, we're such good *teachers*. In fact, most of us are excellent teachers. It's when we come to learning, we are dire. Execrable. Excellent teachers and terrible pupils."

"Sadly," I said, "that may well be the epitaph written on mankind's tombstone. Because that is his signature on his own death certificate. Zeus was so impressed by the mentor, Chiron, that he honoured him by making him into a constellation: Sagittarius, in fact. Zeus might have done better by mankind had he so honoured the best pupil."

Ulm took up the baton. I was relieved. I was more tired than I had imagined – and it stopped him, for a moment or two, sucking on those grapes. "'Honour thy father and mother' is also an invocation to honour life," he said. "Therefore to honour yourself. And therefore to parent yourself. And therefore also to honour yourself for being the father and mother _of_ yourself.

"There has been no parent in history who hasn't needed her offspring themselves also to do some of their own parenting. The best parents know that, and encourage their children also to parent themselves. Two parents and a child who must parent herself. Three in one again, no? Is that coincidence? And one in three."

* * *

The next day it was Saskja who came to see me. Well, Saskja came to see _you_, in fact. But I was a good pretext. She also brought grapes! God, all these 'healthy' treats, anyone would think I were sick! What's wrong with _unhealthy_ treats once in a while? That I know of, Buri's is still making tsifalla.

We talked about nothing till you came. And after you came too, for a bit. I remember you small-talked your way into giving her Italian lessons – in fact, rather than just as an empty offer. But it's more than that, isn't it? Maybe you also need some kind of younger sister.

Is that what you are to me? At one level, I suppose. But at another it is something completely different. Akin to soul-sisters, at that level. And at yet another, it is maternal – often, though, I think it is you mothering me.

I can't even now remember how it is we returned to the ten Commandments. We'd arrived at the sixth.

"I have been told that 'Thou shalt not kill' should more correctly be translated as: 'Thou shalt not murder'," I said. "Butchers do not murder, it is argued. And states cannot: War is therefore not murder, nor is capital punishment. That all smacks to me (for all its historical accuracy) of lawyerese – perhaps a lawyerese of the time, but lawyerese nevertheless: semantic chess – clever but not pertinent. And known not to be pertinent. The Commandment seems absolutely clear, and completely unequivocal. It might even be Buddhist, except that I'm under the impression Buddhism doesn't 'command' anything, it 'suggests'.

"Meat does pose a moral dilemma to me. Because I don't like the idea that my nourishment requires other beings to be slaughtered. But the picture enjoyed by some vegetarians that, without meat consumption, there would be herds of ecstatic moo-cows frolicking idyllically, and flocks of fluffy baa-lambs skipping amongst a verdant countryside, sadly is complete fantasy. Overwhelmingly, the majority of animals killed for meat are alive only as a consequence. They have been bred for that reason: to be killed. If we continue to overfish the oceans, that will shortly also be true of fish – at least, of those species which can be farmed. So the more pertinent question vegetarians need to ask of themselves is this: Is the experience of life worth a bloody death?

"For me it is," I said – or did I admit that? "Indeed, there have been times in my life when I have envied beef cows. They seemed to have a purpose in their lives which mine lacked. Oh, I love my children deeply. *My* world is vastly better for their presence in it, and I have to hope that is true too of the world as a whole. But at such moments of crisis, mothering them was not sufficient reason for me to have expended the natural resources which my living had required. And at such times, the idea – frankly – was quite appealing that my carcase could be used to good effect.

"Over no aspect in our lives are we more powerless – yet another of life's ironies – than in our choice of whether or not to be born. Oh yes, I know, I've heard them too," I said in anticipation of the interruption I could see stuttering on your lips, "the theories that we somehow 'choose' our parents. And I have some sympathy for the concept of reincarnation. But that we *know*, in nothing do we have less choice than in the matter of our birth. And abortion *is* an issue here, let's make no mistake about that either. Indeed so is contraception. And they do need to be thought about. But let's not get side-tracked for the moment."

"That'll be a first," you asided, your face po'd, your whisper staged. Saskja laughed rather more loudly than, suddenly, she realised was polite. She clamped a hand over her mouth, gawkily, but the smile leaked either side of it, and was anyway burnished in her eyes.

I was trying to be still. Whatever the angle of your head, that neck-brace seems to bite into you. And there weren't too many contortions either where I wasn't aware of the surgeon's recently inflicted wound. Comfortable positions, in other words, were rare. When I found one I was therefore anxious to stay in it. So when I tried to look fiercely at both of you, I lacked the neck to be able to do so, and in very short order you could both call my bluff.

"I think we want to have a chocolate-box view of Nature," I continued. "We want hedgehogs to be Mrs Tiggeywinkle and water-rats to be Ratty. And I think the desire for that chocolate-box view is even more trenchant than our having it. We know orcas kill baby whales but we hate watching it. We prefer not to think about cheetah cubs being torn apart by baboons or barn owls cannibalising their own young. But when we gaze at Nature through rose-coloured binoculars – or through selective binoculars – we distort her. There is *nothing* sentimental about Nature. She is a harsh goddess. And to venerate her as a goddess without recognising her harshness is not veneration, but blasphemy. It is the worship not of truth, but of fantasy.

"Again, there is – in its place – nothing wrong with fantasy. Provided it is accepted as being such. When we start believing, though, fantasy is reality, we are in grave danger. We start – again – worshipping a cherub in our pantheon as if it were a god. And that must lead to disappointment and disaffection. So we stop believing in the pantheon at all.

"Killing for meat is common amongst mammals – and amongst fish, for that matter, and insects, invertebrates, amphibians, the whole kit and caboodle.

"Maybe we will grow into a vegetarian species. We're certainly not one yet. And, that being the case, I fear that vegetarians (who are – let there be no mistake about that – mostly good people, and kind people, and admirable people) … I fear that they may divert our eyes from the real atrocity: the way in which so many of our farmed animals live and the processes which constitute their slaughter.

"It should, I think, be a requirement that our children visit poultry and beef farms. They should be taken," I said, "to abattoirs. On field trips. Great long crocodiles of them. Not 'city' farms, or cosmetic farms – not the equivalent of those model 'concentration camps' the Nazis built so that the Red Cross could visit them. Real farms, I'm talking about. Working, no-frills, no-veils veal farms. Likewise just any abattoir.

"Children would be appalled. Let's let that famous 'nag factor' work for once on behalf of something humane, and not just be induced further to inflate the toy manufacturers' already vast profits."

"It would be argued," said Saskja, "that we can't afford it: humane animal slaughter, I mean."

"And there are others," you added, "who would consider humane slaughter an oxymoron."

"And they've both got points," I said. "Good points have been made throughout history. Read some of the arguments tended against Wilberforce when he was trying to abolish slavery, or against Lincoln by the Confederates, or against Mrs Pankhurst when she was fighting for the vote. If something is morally wrong, it is wrong. Morality is not the servant of economics. Morality is the God of the First Commandment, economics is but another of those cherubs we worship mistaking it for a god. It should be ethics, not economics, the master of our household. Ethics should dictate *to* economics, not be dictated to *by* them.

"The economy did not collapse because slavery was abolished. Or because women started voting. It wouldn't collapse if we farmed our animals with compassion and slaughtered them with concern. Our feeding habits may change. There may be fewer farm animals in the world. But we could eat with a clearer conscience."

"I see there's escalope on the menu for supper," you said, with a tacit wink of complicity at Saskja.

"I'm having the fish," I replied. "That's still killing, of course. Of course, that's still killing. And I'm very not-crazy about the idea. I already said that. I simply prefer it to the alternative. Where vegetarians, vegans, Buddhists stop, I really don't know. Is it okay to kill a malarial mosquito? If it's buzzing around the children's ward of a hospital? Is it okay to destroy a virus? To wash one's hands?

"I would hope that such would be up to each person to decide. Having said that, I do, I'm afraid, get rather uncomfortable when a person's views can harm an innocent third party. I have no problem with Jehova's Witnesses refusing medical treatment, for example, but I do have a problem when they start declining it on behalf of a child. I would likewise have a problem with someone who refused to kill a malarial mosquito, or a rogue elephant that was about to stampede into a village. Because we have God within us, that does not entitle us to play at *being* God.

"It is without doubt that an incalculable (and intolerable) amount of pain is inflicted on animals because we are too squeamish to check on what is being done to them – and in our name! Of course we must protect the panda and the Siberian tiger and the orang-utan. These are treasures of the world, far more precious than most protected buildings. But shouldn't some of the animal charities also be protecting our farm animals from cruelty? Shouldn't we?

"We tut outside bullrings, then buy a bacon sandwich. And whilst we weep over the death of Bambi's mother, we're munching on hot dogs.

"Vegetarians, I fear, are often the butcher's best friends: They are the illusionist's assistant, the skimpily clad young woman taking our eyes away from what the conjuror doesn't want us to see. It is not the fact of killing animals which is the barbarity, but the manner."

Which was when news reached the hospital of that terrible train crash, and you were summoned immediately to duty. And with equal lack of ceremony – thank God! – I was booted out of bed. It'd be needed, they said, for trauma patients.

You'd already gone, but Saskja – God bless her cotton socks – rose to meet the occasion. Splendidly, in fact. Like some kind of nursing Neptune, rising from the sea. She phoned her father, asked him to come to the hospital, drive me home. She anticipated the chaos it was going to be downstairs, and arranged a rendezvous outside the grounds. She walked me all the way along that long corridor – remember? – down the stairs. There was an old woman hogging the corridor as she slouched towards us. Saskja simply dribbled me round her, like I was a basketball or something. She didn't try to hurry me, didn't buy in either to the flap and barely controlled panic all around us. She was the tortoise in a March of hares – no, even more than that, she allowed me to be the tortoise.

I know she told you all this, and that we talked about it later. But then you know everything these jottings contain. God, you're most of the time *half* of them! They're there only as an aide-mémoire for you, something you can come back to at a later date and which will help you to think things through. An 'aide-cogitation' may be a better expression, whatever it is, the French for cogitation – which, thinking about it, is probably exactly the same. I also know I've told you before how magnificently Saskja performed. But I have a need to commit that to paper. For those of us who have no possibility of, I don't know, Oscar acceptance speeches or something, no access to being recorded, sometimes a letter or an entry in our diary is our only way of making 'public' some private act of kindness or of courage.

Saskja, for that record, was both kind *and* courageous. The entrance to the hospital was a scene from Dante: the sirens wailed and doubly loud, it seemed, as if they were also doing the wailing for the victims, who were still struck dumb by shock or horror or both; passers-by were wheeling gurneys because the porters were gathering from the ambulances a pick 'n' mix of severed limbs; the newly-arrived victims smeared bright red stripes of blood across their t-shirts, mixed with jet-black oil. Perfectly sighted people were groping blindly for any structure to support them, their eyes misted over by revulsion or grief or disbelief.

She'd known, Saskja, it would be bad, had guessed, for instance, her father would never get through such a maelstrom. But nothing had prepared either of us for the reality of what we saw there. Age somehow inures you to horror, though. Suddenly, Saskja was as old as I was. Still allowing me my carapace and my plodding, she steered me to that intersection by the haberdasher's. We waited by the café there. There was something surreal, amidst all the surrounding mayhem, about the way those chickens kept turning on their rotisserie. Like a dove settling on a trench at the Somme. Even more surreal was the arrival of the old fiddler, scraping out some kind of ludicrously malapropos ... well, jig, I suppose it was.

I was wilting. And fast. And I hated the fact that I wanted to moan about that, and knew I couldn't. But I wouldn't berate myself for that either. Oh, I know I'm a really selfish old bat, but I also know that, for all but saints, in pain our first priority is to get out of it! I will no longer berate myself for being human. Maybe I've finally learnt that I do not need to feel shame because (privately!) I fart.

It seemed to be interminable, the wait for Saskja's father. I tried to tell myself I had nothing to complain about, but I didn't really believe me. You can't, of course, see the hospital entrance from that intersection, but the flow of traffic – and of human traffic – was remorseless. And, actually, only added to my pain. I heard later that children had been killed. Thank God I didn't see that.

Which, I suppose, is an almost perfect example of what I had been trying to talk about earlier. Somehow we have this amazing facility, us humans, to believe that if we don't see it, it isn't happening. Lumps of meat wrapped in cellophane aren't the remains of animals; ambulances carrying the corpses of children are vehicles that are *saving* lives.

If we are going to do something to check horrors, we've simply got to insist of ourselves that we see them. And when governments seek to 'protect' us from such sights, we've simply got to not let them.

We cannot, Giselle, simply condemn God-the-Holy-Ghost as if that were not – at least, in part – created by God-the-Son. We cannot condemn the God of a godless world without examining the godlessness that, like God, also nestles within us. We cannot stand in judgement of the Holy Ghost without also standing in judgement of God the Son – *our* God, in other words, the God which is partially contained in us – to see how much responsibility *we* have, each one of us, for creating or condoning that Holy Ghost.

It is said of Vietnam that it was the first televised war – and the last! That thereafter the military (of whichever nation) has been extremely careful about the images it allows to be seen by the audience back home. I think we owe it to ourselves as human beings (and as a member also of an endangered human race) to protest vociferously about such censorship. If abominations are being perpetrated in our name, we should not only be allowed access to such sights, we should insist that we witness them.

We should, I think, be required to witness state executions. And if such excites the cruel in us, the callous, the voyeur, the ghoul, then that too is a distressing spectacle which we owe it to ourselves to witness. You do not address the disagreeable within you by pretending it doesn't exist. That is – you ask Ezekiel – the denial of the junkie.

There are no aspects about capital punishment which don't appal me – including, usually, the crime or crimes which have occasioned it. I say 'usually' because it is only a remarkably short time ago that a playwright was hanged merely for protesting about the rape of his country by oil corporations. Not long before that, a young princess was beheaded for adultery – a 'crime' which still in Iran today for women carries the death penalty.

Tolstoy never recovered from seeing a public execution, but history also testifies to the crones knitting beside the guillotine, and the festival atmosphere that pervaded at many public hangings. We don't become more civilised by hiding our barbarities. We become civilised only by acknowledging them. And then seeking to foreswear them.

God, Giselle, we were talking to Saskja only a few days before this about what nice people the Italians are. The Italians are direct descendants from those who drooled as gladiator smote gladiator and Christians were mauled by lions. Were the Romans the aberration of the ancient world? Or was the Mr Hyde in them let loose with the sanction of the status quo? Less bread and *circus* than bread and *psychosis*.

Perhaps there is within the God-the-Son of all of us a lust for the macabre, a schadenfreude bordering on the psychopathic – or simply a desire for someone to be in a worse place than we are. If that is the case, let's expose that aspect of ourselves, let's get it out of the closet, that we might start dealing with it.

Freud's theory about the Oedipus complex did not, so far as I know, induce a spate of either patricide or incest. Indeed I suspect that those who are able to progress beyond their initial snicker and/or revulsion have better relationships with their parents than they would otherwise have done. Our faults and our vices are never more dangerous than when we are trying to deny them. It seems to be that the denial strengthens them. Certainly strengthens the grip they have on us.

I do not believe the mentally fit suffer from any condition that cannot be addressed – not always removed, but certainly reduced. But I am *certain, absolutely* certain, that no problem ever got solved by pretending that it wasn't a problem. And no vice, peccadillo, peculiarity, phobia, psychosis – or even mild eccentricity – was ever tackled without it first being recognised.

The drive home was also interminable. That many emergency vehicles on the street just have to cause anarchy. No complaints there: in such disasters seconds can sometimes be the difference between life and death. Considerably less acceptable was the way that so many un-emergency drivers were compounding that anarchy by trying to drive in the slipstream, as it were, of the ambulances. Thereby delaying those ambulances behind the first. What would those drivers have been saying, I wonder, if it had been they or their loved ones in those ambulances now gridlocked by such selfishness?

When finally we did get back to my flat, Saskja insisted on staying. Her father told her (if he ever got home!) he'd be back to fetch her later that evening. I tried to insist she went with him then. To be completely frank, I really wanted to be alone. Oh, I love Saskja, you know that. But I was achy and cranky and tired and unhappy with myself and extremely hot and even more bothered … almost menopausal all over again!

I slept, though. Saskja demanded that I sleep. And when I woke, I found she'd placed on my bedside table a fan which blew its air over a bowl of cut lemons she had prepared. She'd been reading in that wicker chair by the bed. She brought me some mint tea, washed my face with that little yellow guest towel. She is such a special person.

She made sure I was comfortable. Then asked – she'd clearly been stewing about it all afternoon – if the circumstances existed in which I would kill. And I told her there were. If someone I loved were in extreme pain, I told her. She asked me to discount euthanasia. Yes, I said, even then: if she were threatened, say. Or you were. If any of my family was, any of my friends. I doubted, I told her, I'd be too happy with myself for having done so – but, even knowing that, I would still kill. It is, however, none but a tiny percentage of those killed who are killed for that reason.

"I would even," I confessed to her, "have fought in a war. In the Second World War, anyway. Even with hindsight. In fact, I think *especially* with hindsight. The complete, unmitigated atrocity of what Hitler was doing even outweighs 'Thou shalt not kill'. I'd have been ready to kill – even if I'd had to go to Hell for doing so. And if I hadn't done so directly, I'd have been ready to do so vicariously. Munitions workers also kill.

"But it is important to ask ourselves questions too about that war. Have we learnt its lessons, for instance? Have we even learnt that that war was caused because we hadn't learnt the lessons from previous wars?

"So many atrocities came to their head in World War Two: the consequences of human idolatry, of militarism and poverty, of racism and scapegoatism and censorship. History screamed (still screams) at us the consequences of all these aspects of our personality, and to an extent which beggars description. And so, because we are such great pupils, we have, right?, learnt. We have ensured, haven't we?, that the circumstances do not exist where the atrocities of the Second World War could happen again.

"Like Hell we have.

"We still have human idolatry. Those running for President or Prime Minister still seek demigod glory. And that's not a lesson we have failed to learn from Hitler, but from Caligula! So many of the political conferences we see today and conventions differ mostly from Nuremberg – and imperial Rome – only in degree and grandiosity.

"Censorship? It is a more covert censorship we exercise today. It's exercised, most of it, under the guise of 'free speech' and exists in the control of the media that is enjoyed by a handful of plutocrats. What are spin 'doctors' … (which is already a deception. 'Doctor' gives such deceivers a credibility they most certainly are not entitled to. Spin 'jockeys' maybe would be a better name for them. Or spinmen, soul-brothers of conmen.) … what are these spin 'doctors' but Goebbels without a final solution? And with twenty-first century tools?

"We see every day the growth of militarism. The end of the Cold War has done nothing to alleviate that – has not by *one jot* done anything to alleviate that. There are more destitute and starving people, more people living in real poverty now than in the 1930's.

"As for racism … Why did we tolerate apartheid for so long? Australia's immigration policy? The Jim Crow Acts? The imprisonment of American Civil Rights' leaders? Why do there continue to be race riots in England and in France? What about Israel's racist policies? *Israel's*, for heaven's sake? It's hard to credit. What about the tribalism of African countries, and the genocides that have occurred as a consequence? Tribalism is only racism in another form. So is sexism. Where are the protests from the powerful countries against those countries, often their allies, who continue to treat their women as second-class citizens?

"And scapegoatism? It's all around us. It's now the war on terror. It has been the Iron Curtain, junkies, illegal immigrants, the Trades Unions, homosexuals, atheists. The Falklands' war was entirely a scapegoat war.

"And at the end of the Second World War, how well did we look at ourselves? Or did we do the usual victors' trick of blaming all the excesses on our enemy? It was a peculiar German sadism responsible for Auschwitz, a Prussian arrogance which had started the war, a Japanese cruelty which allowed for the excesses in their prison-camps.

"Concentration camps were the invention of the British. Communal punishment we condemned in the Germans, yet the British again used it in Malaya, and the Americans in Vietnam. Our failure to look at ourselves has led to us today using Gestapo methods on prisoners in Iraq, and the use of wholesale torture by U.S. troops, with U.K. complicity, in Guantanemo Bay.

"The genocides of millions have occurred in the Balkans, in Africa and Asia. Dictators have seized power throughout the globe. Fifty million were killed in the Second World War. That's almost the entire population of the United Kingdom. Because we have so totally failed to learn its lessons, I'm willing to bet that a fairly similar number has been killed by bellicose action *since* then. Not least because it is so very much in the interest of so many arms' manufacturers that this should be so.

"To the extent we are told our economies depend on that industry.

"What are we doing?

"Again?

"Giving paraffin and matches to the pyromaniac. Rendering unto Caesar, in an obscene and blasphemous manner, that which is God's. And this is in total contravention to 'Thou shalt not kill'.

"It won't be easy to avoid war. It's become entrenched in the thinking of those deciding foreign policy. It's still an option. And for the inadequate Premier or President, it is a way that he thinks he will guarantee his place in the shorter history books. Or that she does.

"War has already created so much hostility that pervades the planet today. The economic and cultural wars daily create so much more. But if we, as a globe, are going to make a commitment to *try* and stop it, certainly national economies have to stop needing such sales for their buoyancy.

"But, alongside that, each of us has to make a commitment to visit those parts of ourselves where we feel most uncomfortable. The man who hasn't met his rapist does not fully know himself, nor the woman who has not met her whore. Neither does either of them who hasn't met their Auschwitz guard or their murderer or kidnapper. (Not, you understand, that I'm equating being a whore with being a rapist, a murderer or an Auschwitz guard. In any other way, except that it is an aspect of ourselves most of us women do not like to look at.)

"We have to know these 'not nice' parts of ourselves to protect ourselves from them – both individually and as a society. Jekyll's tragedy was less that he 'created' Mr Hyde than that, having done so, he did so little to restrain Hyde's activities. Finding our Hyde is not a license to let him rampage; it is, rather, giving substance to a ghost and thus enabling us to tether him.

"It's not good enough simply to blame government. We have to sweep our side of the street. If we do get to know us the street-walker, us the torturer, there will be a new climate abroad. And that climate will be irresistible, even to government. The world does change because of social climate. And it changes too if we're honest – even if the only person we're honest with is ourselves.

"Do we really want better schools? Or would we prefer to have the cash? We may detest the government's health policy, especially when we hear of children dying because of it, but are we actually prepared to foot what would be an enormous bill to pay for a good one? How often do we want our political cake and eat it? Or our social or economic cake?"

"Does that apply, do you think, also to abortion?" Saskja asked. "This 'cake-and-eat-it' argument? And to contraception? You said you'd return to it later," she added by way of explanation.

"My problem with those who argue against contraception – and, in the age of AIDS, 'prophylactic' is now a more accurate term – is my problem with Jehovah's Witnesses or Christian Scientists who refuse medical treatment: If it is God's decision whether or not we live or die, who is to say that God's decision is not manifested by the presence of medical expertise? Or birth control? If God is omnipotent (a view I personally disagree with, but my view here is not the issue), how is it not that God is not saying, 'I want you to live so much I have given you these doctors to make you well'? Or 'I so do not want these sperm to fertilise that I have given you the means to avoid insemination'?

"Giselle and I talked about sex and procreation," I said.

Sakja said, "She told me about it."

"It's one of those arguments, that against contraception," I continued, "which I simply do not understand. I find it offensive, in fact, but only insofar as those who forward it also claim some kind of moral high-ground. On no authority whatsoever except their own. But such authority, they feel, entitles them to terrorise others also into subscribing to their belief.

"Abortion is a more vexed question. I completely refute the allegation, tacit within the nomenclature, that to be 'pro-choice' is to be 'anti-life'. I have to be a little bit careful here, because on the whole I'm not too wild about the politicians who oppose abortion. And that dislike can blind me to the arguments of those essentially good people who share – on this issue, at least – those politicians' views.

"Finally, though, the argument around abortion *is* about choice.

Those who sanction legal abortion are not *advocating* it. I've never heard anyone claim yet that it is a suitable means of contraception. I've also known no-one who has been happy about having one.

"I would like to see, Saskja, those who demand the right to life, the so-called 'pro-lifers', also protesting about economic policies and health policies that are likewise confiscating life. Without those demands, their calls sound to me less 'pro-life' than 'anti-sex'. And to be anti-sex is to be anti-life. Unequivocally."

* * *

You were exhausted. Your eyes just wanted to curl up under their lids and snuggle into rest. You'd worked almost without a break for two-and-a-half days. You'd seen terrible things, things the witness of which is almost as traumatic as their experience. And yet, for all their exhaustion and for all their recent experience of horror, there was sheen in those eyes, a glow.

I thought initially that was to do with saving lives, with mollifying pain or soothing misery … maybe with feeling useful. And it *was* all those things. Despite what you say, it was, at least in part, *all* those things. You made coffee – "to keep me awake" –, you blushed more deeply than I'd ever seen you – you blushed purply! – and blurted that the glow was to do with Rodolfo.

Rodolfo, you said, was a Peruvian, now living in London. A thoracic surgeon. He'd been on holiday here. With his English wife and children. He'd heard about the crash, had rushed to the hospital to volunteer his services. Some kind of *überdoctor*, you thought him, some kind of *wunderquack*. The injured ceased being the injured, and became a litany of patients on whom the *wunderquack* had wrought his miracles. If all the doctors in London were like Rodolfo, you garbled, maybe I should go *there* for treatment. And maybe, you blushed again, you should accompany me there. What you could learn from such doctors!

And not only a *wunderquack*, but a *wunder*man, to boot. Such a kind man, you said, such determination mixed with such sensitivity … such a good-looking man. Adonis with a stethoscope. To the bedside manner born, and born too with come-to-my-bedside eyes. As you described him, so the fatigue sought to lift. As if Atlas's globe were trying to fill itself with helium. It couldn't, however. It was too heavy. But, like an eagle with a broken wing, though it could not soar, it could flap in the expectation of soaring. And you became Saskja's age, all a-fluster about your first date – lots of awkward and inverted hand-clasps, lots of coy chins nestling on the collar-bone, lots of upturned eyes and arms windmilling … and gawkiness and angst.

If only, you kept saying, he weren't married. If only, you kept protesting (like the lady, too much), you weren't involved with Ezekiel. Not that he'd even noticed you, you kept saying. Gawkily. Angst-riddenly.

The heat that day was suffocating. It seemed less to have sucked the air out of the atmosphere than to have siphoned it out. There was, though, not a bead of sweat on you. As if memory of Rodolfo were a gentle gust – the breath, maybe, on a kiss of life … maybe, on a kiss of love.

And then suddenly your windmills ran out of wind, and the kite you were flying ran out of sky, and you sat heavily on the couch as I described to you *my* last two days. You kicked off your sandals, and sprawled lengthwise on the couch, and you cupped your chin in one hand, and supported it on your elbow. Within seconds you were asleep. Even perched like that. Deeply asleep. I had to re-arrange you.

That was at about seven. When I went to bed, just before eleven, you were still asleep, still where you were when I'd arranged you. I don't think you'd so much as shuffled since then. I was therefore amazed the next morning when I went to make my usual coffee at my usual seven-thirty, to find that you had gone. You'd left a note, I'm sure you remember, to say you'd be back later.

I thought 'later' meant later that day. It was another three days before I saw you again. Rodolfo was still working at the hospital. He'd indeed obtained some kind of leave-of-absence from his

London hospital in order to help with the emergency, was staying on another three weeks. His family, though, had returned.

All was not quiet on Rodolfo's matrimonial front. He'd hinted at that, and then had wanted to know more about *you*. He'd noticed you wore no ring, but a lot of women didn't these days: were you married? No, you'd told him. "Involved with someone?" You'd replied, "Not really." Well, you weren't, you insisted. Not – you insisted – *really* involved. Ezekiel, you'd always told me – so you said – was a stud more than a lover. You had been looking, you said, not for love but for sex. So, it was true, wasn't it? What you'd told Rodolfo. That with Ezekiel you weren't *really* involved. Well, *of course* involved, but not *really* involved, as you put it. I fudged some sort of non-comment, and we quickly moved on to a more neutral this 'n' that.

You suggested a walk, but I wasn't up to it. It would have been a lovely evening for it: Orphalese on those balmy days of summer surely is Paradise on Earth. As it was, the zest of the Seville orange-trees sailed in on that whispered breeze. And that breeze melted the iron gauntlet of the sun into a kitten-furred mitten.

"You're avoiding the subject," you told me. We were eating the lentil stew that I find delicious, and you edible. You'd indulged me. It *was* winter fare, I knew that, but I'd developed a craving.

"I am?"

"The seventh Commandment," you said.

"Not avoiding it," I protested. And I hadn't been. I'd merely not forced an issue I thought you might want to avoid.

"'Thou shalt not commit adultery'."

"Pity," I said.

"Pity?"

"It's a lot more fun, adultery, than killing."

"You say that from personal experience?"

"I have very little experience of killing."

"And adultery?"

"The odd fly, perhaps. I eat meat. I do kill vicariously. We already talked about that."

"And adultery, Lakshmi?"

"The reason, Giselle, it's called a private life is because it is: private. There is that, apparently in all of us – evidently in you, and, yes, certainly in me – which loves to gossip and to speculate. 'Is Joan having an affair with John?' kind of thing. 'Has Lakshmi committed adultery?'," I added pointedly! "And I'm sure most of us have occasionally wondered what antics a couple gets up to in the bedroom. I don't find that a very attractive aspect of the human condition. It is, if you like, the unacceptable face of curiosity. The private should be allowed to remain private. That's how we show respect for our fellow creatures, that's an important way in which we recognise their dignity. But I do accept that the hunger for the salacious, for the prurient does seem to be something innate to us, almost invincible.

"I have no problem – well, not many – with erotic novels, or with the erotic *in* novels. That's fiction. It is perfectly acceptable to invade the privacy of fictitious characters. But I do have problems with 'kiss-and-tell' interviews in the press. Personally, I think such pandering debases us far more than the ogling and being-ogled involved in pin-up photography, where all parties are complicit in what is occurring. Sex, it seems to me, is not only the most loving form of intercourse, but also the one in which most trust is invested. The betrayal of trust is not something which should ever be encouraged.

"I *am* talking about adultery, Giselle," I said. "It's all inter-twined, this whole thing. Is it not precisely the betrayal of trust which is one of the chief pains of adultery?"

"And I am listening, Lakshmi," you said, collecting the plates, stacking them in the sink. "I didn't realise I needed to signal to you that I was."

"Sorry," I said. You acknowledged the apology with a worn out smile. "It's yet another handicap, Giselle, of getting old. We repeat ourselves so often, even when we're not, we think we might be."

"Go on," you said. You went to the fridge, got out the figs. Started peeling them.

"We talked, Sakja and I, about abortion," I said.

You said, "I heard," and, mid-peel, went to the fridge again for the goat's cheese. The honey you got from the shelf. You didn't say any more. And I didn't pursue it.

Instead I continued, "Like abortion, pornography and prostitution have always been there, and I suspect always will be. Drive it under cover, and the people who most benefit are the pimps ... the knitting-needle abortionists ... the crooks. And the first people to suffer will be the whores, the porn models, and the pregnant. My preferring that none of these things existed is not going to affect the reality of their existence. Not by one iota.

"And there is an argument which indicates both pornography and prostitution reduce the instances of violence against women. And that has got to be a good thing. (Though it also must be said that the biggest problem with argument today is that so much data is manipulated – and by both sides. We really never know the truth. This is not free speech. This is, and its advocates know it, an abuse of free speech.)

"I'd prefer that whores and porn models would – and, much more importantly, *could* – earn their money in a different way. But then I'd prefer boxers not to box and matadors not to fight bulls and cullers not to club baby seals to death. I wish there weren't bailiffs or debt-collectors or hangmen ... or commodity brokers. Those involved in pornography are, at least, doing something which is essentially pleasurable to, and with, other people. I'd certainly rather watch a couple copulating than slugging each other into a coma.

"If there *is* choice involved, I think I must respect that choice. I think, in a way similar to abortion, the principle of choice outweighs my discomfort with the existence of these things.

"Pornography is just prostitution made public, and prostitution, apart from all its other attendant difficulties, is so hard to define: Is the actress kissing her stage husband prostituting herself? What is the model on the cover of a fashion magazine but a stripper with her clothes on? The wife who succumbs to her husband as the line of least resistance, is that woman a whore? Kings when they arranged political marriages for their princess daughters, were they not just pimping them?

"It's when there is *no* choice that I can, and must, object. Physical or economic coercion, it's pretty much one and the same. A hungry family selling their daughter into bondage is, of course, acting wickedly. Not least because this too is a betrayal of trust. And it is without question that the pimp 'buying' such a girl is acting wickedly.

"But the true wickedness is an economic reality which makes such actions inevitable. That's the real obscenity, the true obscenity: The poverty which calls these people to whoring themselves. Calls them to it? Yells them to it, screams them to it."

Silently you passed me the compote. You sat down opposite me. Those grey eyes of yours were leaking with compassion. We both knew women in Orphalese destituted into prostitution. It is a consummation devoutly *not* to be wished.

"It's another area too," I continued, "where men need to look deep inside themselves. A lot of men pay lip-service to their disapproval of prostitution. (So many indeed, I'm forced to wonder how the poor girls scrape together a living!) How many of those disapproving men, though, have availed themselves of such services? Even if only by glancing through a 'girlie' magazine? And of those who haven't, how many – oh, deep, deep down! – *want* there to be hookers, if only as a fail-safe? Or maybe, if only as something they can feel morally indignant about!

"We will change nothing about the fabric of our world, its woof or its weave, unless we get to know ourselves. The Holy Ghost will not be controlled by God-the-Son until God-the-Son gets honest with Himself. Do you not think that's what could have been meant about first removing the mote from our own eye?

"I say 'men', though I understand that now most subscribers to porn television stations are women. Which, if true, goes against some kind of grain – not least that sexologists have been telling us for some time that the female libido is stimulated by imagination and the male by the visual. If it *is* women who are the principle audience, that's alright, let's acknowledge that. And if that goes against the grain, well, let's re-examine the grain.

"But we don't know, of course. It could well be that those figures have been manipulated to avoid the charge of sexism. If there used to be 'lies, damned lies and statistics', there is now a fourth layer which is 'spun statistics'. And that is no longer whimsical or amusing, it is planet-threatening. And it is not, I repeat, free speech, but an abuse of free speech.

"Sex pervades so much of society, so much of government, so much of the way life is organised. And I suspect we seek to snigger at it for the same reason the Church, in its plurality, seeks to debase it: in order to wrest from it some of its power.

"The origins of sexual power are not even, I don't think, pre-historic. I suspect that they pre-date man, that they are to be found in us as apes – maybe even at their *latest*. Oh, I'm certainly no expert – in this as in anything else – but I understand that chimpanzees are, instinctually, polygamous. It is only the alpha male who tries to invoke fidelity among the clan – and not for himself, merely his mates: He wants his to be the only genes passed onto future generations. He is not always successful. But the message is clear: 'Sex equals power'. That is a message which is still today hugely power*ful*. It still pervades, indeed I think it still prevails.

"There seems to be little question that Neanderthal man was, by instinct, polygamous and his female counterpart monogamous – presumably as the consequence of both simian heredity and because an individual male life was, for the survival of the species, a lot less precious than a female one: the Dr Strangelove principle.

"Do we here have a basic conflict between genders? The man who wants to be polygamous, and the woman who wants to be monogamous? Or has woman been duped over thousands of years into *believing* she wants to be monogamous? Interesting the amount of religions which permit, even advocate, polygamy for the male and not for the female.

"Ask a straw poll of the population which of the two sexes is most likely to agree with the tenets of this seventh Commandment ('Thou shalt not commit adultery'), and my guess would be that, strongly, it would be women. And yet this would seem to be a trap for women. Far from liberating them, it contains them. It also sanctions indolence in the core relationship of one's life.

"Let us mull for a moment, Giselle. Is this Commandment not the thin end of the unfortunate wedge whereby we consider those we love our property, our chattels? And if such is the case, do we not then stop having a partner but a bondsman? Is such not likely to have been a manmade, as opposed to a womanmade, invention? As he left to fight mammoths or wars, did he not want the security that he would return to 'his' partner's loving embrace?

"And the possessive pronoun itself, was that not also likely to have been invented too by man the gender? How much misery and havoc have been unleashed on the world by *that*, by the possessive pronoun? And is this Commandment, if not the start of that possessiveness, at least not furthering its cause? Psychologically when you describe Ezekiel as 'your' lover – your '*stud*', I'm sorry –, how much claim do you then lay on him?

"It's a vexed question. It, rather, invites vexed questions. A whole batch of vexed questions. The whole issue of sex and sexual fidelity invites an encyclopaedia of vexed questions. And if there are *any* answers to those questions, they are only particular ones. There are no answers which apply universally, not even generally.

"The monogamist is certainly not the only person capable of deep romantic love, nor the only person capable of deep parental love. There's very little doubt that children do prefer to be raised by both a father and a mother. But that becomes greatly less the case if either parent is unhappy – or both are. And they certainly do not fare better if, because of that unhappiness, one of their parents turns to violence or abuse. Or both do.

"Good parents come – mostly – from happy people. A happy person usually is one who *decides* to do something, not one who does it because he is constrained to. If you offer to do the washing-up, the chore will be one done with ease. Ordered to do it, each plate will weigh like an anchor."

"I was just going to offer, as a matter of fact, to do the washing-up," you chimed in.

"I was rather hoping," I said, "you might take the hint. But," I added, seizing on the fruit compote you put before me, "I'll let you have your pudding first."

"Too kind," you said. "'Thou shalt not steal', that's going to take us till tomorrow, right?"

"'Thou shalt not commit adultery', I thought we were talking about that."

"There's *more* to say on it?"

"I was going to say that the essence of the seventh Commandment is – again – 'Unto thine *own* self be true'. You see, I don't think it's for anyone else to dictate to a couple how that couple should prosecute its sexual life. What business is it of anyone except the couple concerned? Because couple 'a' wants a monogamous relationship does not mean couple 'b' must have one too. But neither does it mean that because couple 'b' has a polygamous relationship so must couple 'a'.

"A lot of people come to talk to me about their sex lives. I suppose I'm considered a 'safe' person, not threatening like a therapist or someone who might actually be able to tender some positive suggestions. If my experience is the least bit typical, I'd say that overwhelmingly the chief emotion invoked by people's sex life is disappointment. And that's a shame. Oh, not disappointment with the prowess of their partner's performance. That can be a part of it, but it is a considerably smaller part than the time and attention and imagination which that partner is prepared to invest in the overall life they have together, and which comes to be exemplified by the sexual aspect of it.

"A part of that disappointment is inevitable. It's the pornography of fairy-stories, of 'happy ever after', of pop songs: There is an expectation that matches are made in Heaven, that you fall in love forever, that there is nothing more to a relationship than that.

And sex is a large part of that false expectation.

"But it's not the whole story. Considerably more attention is paid to variety in cuisine than coitus. We are very sexual beings, us human beings. Yet sex in so many relationships, after the initial flurry, starts becoming something mundane, predictable … a duty.

"It's been in the closet so long we're only just now starting to talk about it. But most of the talk I also find either puerile or ridiculously pompous: arcane phrases and a school-ma'amy tone-of-voice. A lesson in geology or Egyptology, not sex. And yet I just hate the snickers, the behind-the-hand, behind-the-bike-shed tittle-tattle, as if sex were something shameful or unclean. Is it really beyond our ken to find a middle path where we can talk sensibly and openly about sex without being either coy on the one hand or medical – should I say clinical? – on the other?

"There *is* more openness today about the subject, that much is true. But much of that openness is merely ill-disguised prurience. And that prurience fails to mention the dangers of sex. Not those of sexually transmitted diseases – those are the easier dangers to handle. No mention is made of the *emotional* minefield we enter when we become sexually involved with a person, however casual we may think that involvement.

"And, more importantly even than that, no mention is made of sex as a drug, as a form of escape, as the addiction it can become if it is used for that purpose. Like narcotics, it can, sex, produce a respite from reality.

"People are in big pain around sex. *Big* pain. Disappointment, were it nothing more serious than that, is already a big pain. And often there *is* more to it than that: impotence or frigidity, for instance, in their hundred different costumes, the use of sex as a tool – or even as a weapon. And the ripple effect of so much pain is, and must be, enormous. We can only guess at the social cost. And, as usual with social cost, the chances are we vastly underestimate it. It's no good you looking at me like that, Giselle. All of this forms part of that Commandment. We cannot talk about 'Thou shalt not commit adultery' without talking about this.

"I've also often wondered, I don't know about you, what 'childery' might be. I mean if 'adultery' is sex with a married partner, what is 'childery'?... Being frivolous, sorry."

"Time out," you said. "Please be frivolous. Let's both be frivolous. I need some time, Lakshmi, to think. To mull, probably I should say. I'm not going to say meditate, but I need time to do something, I'm not sure what, between mulling and meditating. I'm stifling. Do you think I could take a shower?"

"You have no need to ask," I told you. "Remember, sometimes you have to wait for the hot water."

"Another metaphor for life?" you asked and smiled. "I've never talked to Ezekiel, you know, about fidelity, all that."

"We don't," I replied. "We think it's tacit. We don't talk about such things. We're uncomfortable around them. We'd prefer to believe the other person believes as we do. Normally we only talk about them when it's already too late. When the crisis is upon us. When our views have changed. Or things domestically have become *so* painful, we have decided that anything must be better than this.

"And is this lack of talking, I wonder, an indication of our cowardice? Or of our laziness? Probably, as with so many things, a mixture of both. Abetted by a culture which tells us we have no *need* to talk about such things, that they are completely self-evident. A stance which is almost a syllogism – and as silly as most syllogisms.

"It behoves us to remember that a nonsense repeated often enough may sound like the truth, but it remains nonsense just the same. The Inquisition denounced Galileo, and Victorian clerics Darwin, and with great verve and viciousness. But for all their power and instruments of torture, the nonsense both Inquisition and clerics spouted remained nonsense. There is nothing that does not need to be talked about, nothing in the world that is self-evident – and if there are things which are, then the self-evidence of such things itself needs to be talked about.

"The only thing that can be said with any safety around sex in man is that nothing is certain. Beyond what is certain for the individual on any given day. You haven't talked to Ezekiel about it? Well, maybe your relationship is not at the point when you need to. When it is, talk about it.

"Standards are synonyms for flags only in the dictionary. They are not ribbons to march blindly behind. They are things to be thought about, and considered – and to be discussed as well vocally, and, yes, even argued about.

"And they change. Thank God they change. It's essential that they do change. I hope that Marx visiting one of the gulags might have rewritten great swathes of his work – so that it could not be so grossly misunderstood. Likewise Nietzsche or Luther had they been at Nuremberg. Gandhi once said, 'The truth is as I see it each and every day. Consistency is not my concern.' I'm probably paraphrasing, but that was the gist. It's just such hard work, Gandhi's way. That's why we tend to shy away from it. We are lazy, us human beings. And often we hide our laziness behind hard work. It's a good hiding-place for it. It's a lot less taxing working hard, than looking inside ourselves.

"Thinking about it, I think too there's a large part of the fourth Commandment at work here, keeping the Sabbath holy. We need time to consider our moral positions, our principles. Are they still valid? How has reality affected them? Are they still whole, or do they need modifying?"

"That shower?" you asked.

"You know where the towels are," I replied.

"Know something?" you said winsomely. "It feels like I know nothing at all."

"Then," I told you, "you have already learnt a lot."

* * *

I suppose now it's official. Officially now, I suppose, I'm sick. Really sick, I mean. Does that mean, I wonder, that officially now I'm allowed to feel sorry for myself? I do, I'm afraid. A bit. Not all the time. I'm an old woman. And the pain in my life – God, I know it – has been so much less than that most people have to support. Which means that now pain *is* a part of my life, I shouldn't complain. I keep telling myself that. I have no *right*, I keep telling myself, to complain. But I do complain – to myself, at least. Pain is pain, I think, and (I think too I've said this before) when we're in it, the most urgent thing in the world is for us to be out of it – the pain, I mean, not the world. Though, if the pain gets too bad … Well, I just find the idea that euthanasia is in most countries illegal to be yet another instance of man's inhumanity to man. It's amazing what some law-makers find to be covered by the aegis of 'Thou shalt not kill' and what isn't.

'Pain', it's such a little word, isn't it? Such an apparently innocuous word? Yet it's maybe the biggest word in the world. Bigger even than sex. And, again even more than sex, it's probably also the biggest taboo.

Physical pain, that's the easiest type of pain to deal with. Which could be why we concentrate so many resources on it. But there's also mental pain, psychological pain, emotional, intellectual and spiritual pain – and various sub-divisions of all those pains too. It's just as necessary, maybe even *more* necessary, to deal with these pains. But much more difficult.

What they all share in common, these pains, is that they can be separated into two groups: those that can be removed and those which can only be eased. Yes, you're right, Giselle, all of this, it's all obvious. *So* obvious, you're right. It's just peculiar, isn't it, that all these oh so obvious things, we so rarely see them being applied? Why is that?, I wonder.

So, accepting that I'm stating the obvious, and sticking with it for the moment: It's clearly not a pleasant place, pain. Equally clearly, pain is integral to life. But I don't think that means that it is the object of life. Indeed I firmly believe it is our obligation to be as free of pain as we possibly can. Apart from anything else, the less pain we're in, the more care we're likely – and able – to lavish on those around us.

Those pains that we can totally remove, let's do it: Get the tooth pulled or the broken arm reset, see the psychiatrist or the bank manager, the therapist, the lawyer or the priest. Do whatever it takes, and as quickly as we can. Pain is an indication that something is wrong, and the remedy for that kind of pain is to recognise it and to deal with it. It is thus that it is most effectively, most *painlessly*, removed.

And that too we have to recognise: That sometimes the removal of pain is a painful process, and that we need to be as exigent in the control of pain when we are removing pain, as in any other circumstance. A nurse being clumsy with a syringe is inflicting just as much pain as the bouncer manhandling you – or as the straphanger treading on your foot with her stiletto.

And that must be remembered too when we're talking about those other pains – those which can't be removed, only eased. There are many of these, even some physical ones. Arthritis appears to be a chronic condition, rheumatism likewise (although it is also true that for some sufferers these conditions can be brought under a degree of control by complementary medicine – by homeopathy, for instance, or Reiki or acupuncture). My spine is now broken. That is an irreversible condition. Analgesics in such situations help, but they do not cure.

And there are as well chronic emotional pains, chronic pains of all the other types I listed. Grief, for example. Grief never completely leaves you. It gets better, it gets easier, but it never vanishes. Not even in the best of cases. And in the worst ... A loved one's premature death, that can devastate the whole of the remaining life of the one left living – a broken heart likewise, or a broken dream, an unfulfilled ambition. Some people are in chronic emotional pain believing their life unwanted, or feeling out-of-place in it. Some feel very threatened by what they perceive to be a hostile world. And some *are* threatened by it. The wounded wildebeest is not always imagining he's being stalked by a lion.

All these are pains, *real* pains – as real as the wildebeest's sense of danger. But because the world doesn't recognise these *as* pains, those suffering them are coy about them. They keep them secret. They turn, often, to alternative remedies to get them out of the pain: excessive drinking or drug abuse, perhaps. Bullying or a need to control. Compulsive eating or working or exercise or gambling or shopping or sex. Or just being unhappy – usually thereby making everyone else unhappy around them.

The most painless way of dealing with such pain is to go through it.

Sadly, our economies depend on our not going through that pain. Billions are spent persuading us that this product or that service will remove the pain. No, of course they don't say that directly – pain is taboo. But listen to the sub-text. Always listen to the sub-text.

It really doesn't matter how many billboards or television advertisements tell you differently, whatever the problem, you will not feel better simply by buying their wares. Retail therapy is just as toxic a 'cure' for pain as drug abuse – and can lead to problems that are almost as serious. Working too hard likewise. And yet these both now underpin our entire culture.

You will feel better only in one way: by *dealing* with the problem. There is *only* one way to the far side of this kind of pain. You can't go over it, under it, around the side of it, you have to go through it. And – yes, like grasping that tired old nettle – you will find that the greatest pain is the anticipation of the pain: the actual pain, by comparison, is manageable.

I don't think there's any kind of pain that I'm not presently in. A part of it, certainly, is the ridiculous I feel, and the humiliated. Since I was able to walk, I saw one of my principal goals as independence. I have been, in my adult years, even *aggressively* independent. Too much so, I acknowledge that. My relationships have suffered as a consequence – maybe even that with you. I've pushed those away on whom I thought I was becoming too dependent. I think, with hindsight, it's no accident my children travelled the distance they did. Circumstances conspired, I liked to believe. But, whilst I have a vague belief in the concept of kismet and that of karma, I do not believe in pre-destination. It wasn't fate that caused them to migrate, but the inability I had to express the warmth of my love for them.

And I don't believe that God organises anything, not in that kind of a way, not even on an improvised basis. I think there *is* such a thing as pure coincidence. But I also believe that it is then that our psyche or our soul – or a mixture of both – determines how we react to that coincidence. And that's where God does come in – or can come in. It may, in other words, be coincidence that occasions Romeo to meet Juliet. But if he is too shy or she too gauche they will still leave the party separately. And he may need to pray to God for the courage, or she for the poise, to obviate that happening. And it is precisely there I think that God can help, and often does help – more often than not, without our even knowing.

Destiny, in other words, is not pre-destined. It is the zenith of the partnership that Man has with God: it cannot be fulfilled without their mutual support. Nor – and this took me most of my life to realise! – is destiny the future. If your destiny is not the life you are living right now, then – simply – you are not fulfilling it. Sadly, it falls to very few of us to fulfil our destinies. For so many of us because we believe destiny is a goal for tomorrow and not our reality today.

Did I say 'sadly'? So much worse than 'sadly'. It is tragic, one of the tragedies of Man. There are so many tragedies associated with Man. Far too many. But perhaps the saddest of all Man's tragedies is that his tombstone will be inscribed with the saddest of all epitaphs: 'Potential still intact'.

And of course I need to ask myself, as I lie here helpless in bed, is my paralysis my destiny? And maybe the answer is to be found precisely in the powerlessness I now have over that destiny – or my condition. Maybe that is the evidence that yes, it is. I don't think destiny need be a comfortable place – indeed I think it very rarely is. Just as truth is rarely the sponge of the washing-up pad but the scouring-skin on its other side. Nature is not, as I know I've said before, sentimental. Why would we think life is? And if life is not sentimental, why would destiny be? Or truth?

We're involved again with the pornography of fairy-stories. The truth is that very, very few of us live 'happily ever after'. But very few of us ever admit that.

It is yet another form of control: making unhappiness taboo. We are brought up to believe that if we are unhappy, it is we who are responsible. That we are each day as happy as we allow ourselves to be.

And, of course, there's an element of truth in that – as you once said, Giselle, in another context: "… otherwise there wouldn't be a problem"! Of course there is truth in that. Even in Alcatraz there was laughter. Even in Auschwitz. All around me, here in this hospital, there are people in the most hideous pain. Few indeed, even of those, pass a smileless day.

But pain is pain. And there is, contrary to our upbringing, absolutely nothing wrong with saying "ow". There is also nothing wrong with you if you say "ow", nor is there anything wrong with you if that pain causes you unhappiness. And if the unhappiness of others in pain causes *you* pain you are already a part of the solution to the world's problems as opposed to being part *of* those problems.

I agree with Arkona: that life is suffering does not countenance unnecessary suffering. The 'noble truth' recognises the unsentimental nature of life. That does not mean it condones cruelty. Indeed quite to the contrary. I completely agree that its meaning is that there is already enough suffering involved with life and with living. We absolutely do not need to manufacture any more.

And yet we do. The cruelty and the injustice meted out today is even more vicious, because it is recognised as being such. Just as the pollution and the ecological damage we do are the more wanton because now we are aware of the consequences of such actions.

No cruelty, no injustice was ever corrected by people being happy with that injustice. It is so often unhappiness which changes the world. But that unhappiness need not (and this is such a crucial thing to remember) preclude happiness. Again, even in Alcatraz or Auschwitz, the sky was sometimes blue and the sun sometimes shone. Because we are unhappy about one thing does not mean we have to be unhappy about everything. And to believe otherwise again is to allow yourself to be controlled. Governments want you to believe that unhappiness is all-embracing. 'Don't be unhappy,' we have been told since we could walk. 'Your whole life will be so much more miserable.'

A myth also gets propagated that when we are unhappy, it is our fault. Entirely. By that argument the schoolchildren in Hiroshima were responsible for their own mutilation.

We do succumb, some of us, to an all-embracing unhappiness. It's called depression. Most of us, I venture to suggest, have been depressed at some time in our lives. And I'm not talking about feeling melancholy here, or sad. I'm talking about suffering from a sense of fundamental uselessness and hopelessness. There is one real problem with depression (apart from it just being a lousy place to be): It breeds inertia. The inert are a government's absolutely favourite citizens: the mentally inert, anyway, the intellectually, politically, philosophically and – most important of all – *morally* inert. They're so broken they acquiesce – even in their own destruction.

I don't know where the confusion comes from, but there seems to be one, between rage and anger. My late husband, for instance, raged. And rage is noxious. I was frightened when he raged. And distressed. For myself certainly, and certainly for the children. For him? ... Well, that's less sure. Perhaps those rages released pent-up demons. Really, I don't know. I just wish he could have released those demons somewhere else. Not at home, not around the family. My son, I hear tell, also now rages at home. I don't think that is a coincidence.

Rage, as I've said already, is noxious. And, with a few notable exceptions (like the chemotherapy they're dripping into me now), nothing is improved when poisons are brought into the equation.

Anger, though, is empowering. It is a form of pain, and like pain, it tells us when something's wrong. You'll doubtless correct me if I'm mistaken, but I think there is an adage (Buddhist, I suspect), something like 'He who angers you conquers you'. And I know (I think!) what it means, and I think I know the point it's seeking to make. But as a general axiom I don't believe it. He who *enrages* you may conquer you, but that's different. That's rage, not anger.

Anger is normally provoked by being threatened. And it is entirely natural to react aggressively (by which I don't mean violently) if you are being attacked.

Of course these days, we live in so many situations where the simian part of our brain tells us we are under attack when we're not. Being jostled by crowds, for instance. That anger we suppress. Because, if human society is to cohere, we have to. But I do wonder whether the price we pay is not pent-up aggression which we release in other ways – in our business dealings, for instance, or in the way we communicate with our neighbours. I also wonder why absolutely no attempt is made to address this problem. Because it is one which impacts on the entire species. And yet we don't even acknowledge that it *is* a problem. We acknowledge violence as a problem, particularly in urban sprawls, and address it by building more prisons. Which is akin to solving a plumbing problem by building a patio. We may want – even need – a patio. We may scratch our heads thereafter wondering why our drain is still blocked. But blocked the drain will remain. And no amount of patio-building will unblock it. If we want to unblock the drain, we have to unblock the drain.

If we are threatened *politically*, anger is also an appropriate response. Indeed, in a political context, anger is optimism. We get angry politically because we think something could be changed for the better and it's not being. I think the world needs to be recharged with political anger – not with Lenin's anger (which was political *rage*), but with Gandhi's. Or Mandela's. The anger of hatred must lead to violence, it has to. But an anger of love *is* possible. Indeed, if change is to be effected without violence, it has to be born from the anger of love. And if the change is going to be one for the better, it *has* to be effected without violence. Violence else will breed violence.

It's the difference between the Black Panthers and Martin Luther King – though that comparison also begs a difficult question: How much of Dr King's success was due to fear of the alternative?

A huge element of the so-called War on Terror today is the desire – or what is perceived by the executive to be the *need* – to suppress domestic political anger. The erosion of civil liberties which has occurred under the spurious guise of protecting us from terrorism is unprecedented – even in times of war. It has to make us wonder what government is trying to hide from us. What *else*, rather, government is trying to hide from us.

Many of us have allowed this to happen, even disbelieving the (unbelievable) cant which we are daily fed, because of the depression I was talking about earlier. *I* have, now I think back on it. So many of us have been *encouraged* to slip into a deep depression – only to have such depression aggravated by feeling guilty about it! When depressed we are bereft of hope. Those without hope lack energy – to challenge a policy, for example. Even the entire fabric of a policy. Oh God, do governments love the depressed.

It is the angry whom governments fear. Those who realise they can make a difference, that – eventually – governments can only rule with the will of those they govern.

The angry have to be cowed – if necessary, with savaging dogs and shying horses, with gas and bullets and water cannon (all weapons used regularly by governments on their own citizens) – and prison. Prisons are not there to intimidate the law-breakers, but the law-questioners. And those whom governments fear most of all are those, like Mandela or Gandhi or Dr King, who do not fear their prisons and who express their anger in words of love. Those who will not allow government to fragment their cause – because *their* cause, they know, is mankind's. And must therefore embrace the whole of mankind, even those attacking or imprisoning them.

The most hated foe of government today (almost every government in the world, with a very few notable, and splendid, exceptions) is comprised of those who realise there is no such thing as *their* human rights. All human rights are *ours*, all human rights belong to all of us. If one person is deprived of human rights, we all are. Yet another lesson of the Second World War we are today encouraged not to heed!

Governments fear suicide bombers far less than those seeking to build bridges. The concept is not new, 'United we stand ...'. Never has the possibility been greater for international union, and never has division been more manufactured.

Which is scarcely surprising, as the division starts with itself. Government, in its plurality, espouses both globalisation and what it calls 'democracy'. At its core, democracy is about the protection of the one against the many; it is the refuge of the quirky, the eccentric, even the downright unpopular. Globalisation, in essence, is the veneration of the uniform. So, even at a conceptual level, there is conflict.

There isn't conflict within the executive because what they call democracy and what they call globalisation are travesties of themselves. 'Democracy' today (particularly as practised by those countries extolling its benefit) is very rarely democratic. And globalisation has come to mean a boxing match between a heavyweight and a flyweight, where the gloves of the heavyweight have been fitted with horseshoes, where the flyweight has no gumshield, where his boots are lined with lead and his shorts are three sizes too big for him, so one of his hands is constantly occupied in holding them up – and whose coach, like the referee, is on the payroll of his opponent. It represents not the elimination of unfair practise, but the essence of it. There is an argument that it will feed some of the starving, that there will be an alleviation of *desperate* poverty. There is, however, no credible argument that it will not keep the *not-quite* desperately poor *not-quite* desperately poor. It may be a shifting population, that of the not-quite desperately poor, but there will, there has to, remain such a population. One in five of the population in the world's most powerful nation, the architect and sire of globalisation, is born into not-quite desperate poverty.

Wherever we turn, our planet is threatened. And when not our planet, then our species. And everywhere we turn we see problems, not being *addressed*, but being masked. We see tokens being offered, or noises being made. Expensive advertisements urge us not to boil more water than we need. Of course we shouldn't. But as a solution to global warming it is about as significant as sending popcorn to a famine.

If the world's rulers today are indeed our leaders we are being led not to a promised land, but to a land which promises nightmares.

And that is also a pain that I'm in. That is, in fact, the greatest pain. Now that I can no longer walk, I kick myself (or would if I could!) for all those marches I never went on, for all those times I thought to myself, my presence there would make no difference. For all the letters I never wrote, for all the petitions I never signed, for all the times I didn't shout loudly that what I was being spun I knew to be nonsense.

I feel ridiculous, being as helpless as I am. I dropped this pen about ten minutes ago. Not even that could I retrieve. Just a lump, is what I feel I am. A sack of coal. As powerless over my mobility, anyway, as a sack of coal. But less useful. It's my worst nightmare, feeling useless. Feeling that I'm a drain, a burden.

A few years ago, I remember, when it was proved that plants had feelings, the Buddhists needed to assemble a convention. Their philosophy prohibited them from eating 'sentient beings'. Now that sentient beings included plants, on what would they feed? Eventually they decided, so I'm told, that their diet should be restricted to those beings which lacked the power to move. Trout had such power, tomatoes didn't; cows did, but not cauliflowers.

Under which definition, I suppose, a Buddhist could eat me. I wouldn't mind, to tell you the truth. I wasn't kidding about envying cows. I'm not sure how tasty I would be, of course. More gristle these days than meat – and more grizzle, you're saying to yourself, than gristle! I don't know what mutton becomes after it's no longer mutton, but I passed my mutton date ... oh, a while back now.

I also feel ridiculous in anticipation of what I'm about to write. As with so much of this 'journal' (as the Americans would call it), I find myself telling you things you already know. And yet, of course, you don't.

Oh, the events of yesterday will be so ingrained you will be able to recall them on *your* deathbed. And you would swear on all the world's holy books that you remember those events clearly. And you probably do. And yet, however perfectly you may remember them, those events are not mine. One of the Algonquin wits once claimed that the cause of nostalgia was a bad memory. Maybe we're all nostalgic because we, all of us, have faulty memories. It's an unreliable tool, even at the best of times, but it is further blunted by subjectivity, vested interest, egoism – and by a general uselessness amongst us humans at seeing things. Ask any detective, almost the least valuable weapon in his arsenal is the eyewitness account. Often, in such, even the *colour* of the offender is inaccurate, even the gender.

I know you know what happened yesterday, Giselle. And I'm not trying to patronise you by writing about it. I suppose (a bit as I had to for Saskja) I have a need to record it. That's *my* need, Giselle. But also – maybe – it will throw a slightly skewed light for you on those events – skewed for you in the sense they will be remembered from a different vantage point.

He'd already been dead for two days when you got there.

* * *

Thank God the fan was on. In the heat of those days, he would have started to smell. I've heard there are few smells more foul than that of decomposing flesh. I'm happy to take others' word for that. There was no serenity in Ulm's eyes, only horror. As if he had seen waiting for him, not Saint Peter, but the devil. I hope that horror was just the pain of his coronary.

He'd been sitting on that wicker chair. Well, it's the obvious place, isn't it? It's either there or the side of the bed. And we weren't ... well, we weren't there yet with our relationship. It wasn't a sitting-on-the-side-of-the-bed relationship. We'd been talking. But he hadn't really been talking, making noises, no more, gestures – like someone at a dinner party but with tummy trouble, stabbing at the food, not eating it.

I was in bed, of course. Wearing that nightgown, the one with the motif of light blue lilacs – well, of course you know: I was still wearing it when you found me. Thinking back (as, in those forty-eight plus hours I had plenty of time to do), perhaps the décolleté of the neckline revealed too much cleavage. Perhaps it even exposed a nipple. I would have thought myself about as sexy as a mangrove tree rotting into the swamp, but he was certainly (thinking back on it) very distrait. His head was in one place, and his eyes somewhere else altogether.

Suddenly he stood. For no apparent reason. Came to attention, like a sentry outside a palace. Stock still. A toy soldier, rather. Then rigidly he moved towards me. I couldn't think what was happening. It was as though all litheness had suddenly been lifted from his limbs, any kind of suppleness. There was little colour in his face, no movement – not even twinkle – in his eyes. Stiffly he bent over me, I think to kiss me. I would have kissed Ulm. It wasn't revulsion that made me push him away, but ... I don't know ... fear, I suppose. Fear of the unknown. That's what he'd become to me: unknown. Like one of those Hollywood sci-fi epics – you know, where human bodies are possessed by aliens. He was just so strange.

And I didn't shove him away. God, Giselle, you saw me: I didn't have the strength to crack open a boiled egg. Even had I wanted to, I *couldn't* have shoved him away. I just put a hand up to restrain him. It was a request, no more than that, that he would back off sufficiently that I could see his eyes. I needed to see his eyes. The 'push' was a pat. A gentle pat on the shoulder. I barely made contact. But he reeled back as if he'd been struck by a demolition ball.

He collapsed onto the wicker chair, and his eyes glassed over – not in the horror I talked about earlier – but into an abstract and giant question. Just one huge 'why' or something. And he bounced – all very slow motion, this whole thing. Bounced like a billiard ball off a cushion, an in-off off the chair onto the floor.

When I say I leapt out of the bed, I wasn't well. Even then. So the leaping was not that of a startled gazelle, more of a lumbering grizzly bear after a particularly heavy meal. I knew he was dead – which makes what I did so very much more stupid. I knew there was no helping him. There was a *part* of my brain, rather, which knew he was dead. But mine's the brain of a prehistoric beast. Sharks are dead for a couple of hours before their brains let them know it. Even with us, the body does not shut down immediately: our hair and nails continue to grow, for example. Obviously, the news that Ulm was dead was censored by the nail-growing part of my brain from reaching the intelligent part.

I tried to lift him. Like an idiot.

I cannot believe myself. But that's what I did, I tried to lift him.

I heard it crack. The spine. I heard it crack – not like a pistol shot or the lash of a whip, not even like a tumbler dropped onto a tiled floor or two billiard balls striking each other, but like the listless plop of a brick plonked onto cement or a baked potato dropped into a salad. For hours it felt like I was *entirely* paralysed. My whole body, I mean. I wasn't, of course. Not physically. But it felt as though I was. I was immobile. My face inches from Ulm's. As if we'd decided to kiss each other and the moment had been frozen in time, or lava'd like the victims of Pompeii.

I started hating those eyes. Those eyes started sucking everything from mine, and gave nothing back in return. Some giant mosquito not after blood but after the soul. And who siphoned me scoop by scoop, and slurp by slurp. But I was also hypnotised by those eyes, mesmerised by them. It took an effort of the most enormous will to drag my eyes away from his. It was that effort, in fact, which made me realise – finally – that I was able to move at least part of my body. My arms, for instance. I started to lever myself away from Ulm, away from those vampire eyes. You know how heavy your own body is? If you've only your arms to support it?

I eventually got to the bathroom. I decided I would sleep there. I could just about haul myself on and off the loo. The comfort of my sleeping quarters was secondary to my need of that. Thank God it was still warm enough. Heaven only knows what I would have done if it had been during the winter. Well, that's where you found me, of course. God bless you.

My life in the bathroom had been a succession of dozes. You obviously came into the flat during one of them. You say you called out to me. I must have been deeply a-slumber. I was always so exhausted when I did finally manage to drop off, that doesn't surprise me. Your scream woke me. I don't blame you for the scream – of course I don't. How could I? But it's amazing I didn't also have a heart attack. Roused like that from the land of Nod.

And then I called out to you. And you came. You saw me, and you dropped to your knees. And you just hugged me and rocked me and hugged me and cried. And then I cried. Finally I was allowed to cry. I allowed myself to cry. Well, *first* I cried. Then you couldn't get a signal for your mobile in the bathroom. You went onto the balcony to call for an ambulance. And then I sobbed.

I sobbed for so many things. Sobbed because you were there, and because it had taken so long for you to get there; sobbed because Ulm was dead and because I was still alive; sobbed because I knew I would never walk again; sobbed for all the lovers I'd had and, even more, for those I hadn't; sobbed because I was in pain and so was the world; sobbed because I could no longer help myself; sobbed because I was hungry and very frightened; sobbed because when I was three-years'-old my favourite cuddly toy had been mangled by the dog; sobbed because aged six I'd not been allowed to go shopping with my mother. I sobbed for my past, my present and my lack of future – and because I so fear for the future of this planet I leave as my legacy.

And I sobbed, Giselle, because you will be a part of that future, and I won't be around for you when that future wreaks its potential maelstrom. It is you who will be punished for my vices. 'The sins of the fathers ...' – and, oh God, how badly we have sinned, those of us who are about to die.

Your call made, you returned to me and I was still sobbing. And you wanted to know why. No, what am I talking about? You said nothing. *Nothing*. You just held me in your arms, shhed me, swaddled me, pressed me to your breast almost as if to suckle me. And you rocked me gently back and forth, lullabied me with your shhes and your strokes. And I shook with my sobs. As I rattled with them.

It was I, I who wanted to tell you what the sobs were about.

I *kept* wanting to tell you, but the sobs wouldn't let me. They choked the words even as they were forming, squeezed them into husks that became more sobs. I was still sobbing when the ambulance arrived. They are such special people, those paramedics. I need to say that too. Need to commit that to the record.

The sobbing cleansed me. I could not have sobbed, Giselle, without you. Had it been anyone else – even those special paramedics – who had found me, I would not have been able to sob. And the inside of me would have been gunged up like a pipe of Maigret's that had never seen a cleaner, full of ash and slime and shag and spittle, an acrid coating as corrosive to the pipe's fabric as it is revolting to the senses.

As soon as I left your embrace, the sobbing subsided. I don't know whether the paramedics sedated me. I remember them wheeling me into the ambulance, and I remember the doors closing, and I remember feeling both sepulchred and peaceful. A vision of death. No, that's not right either: a vision, rather, of the

moment of death, of how I would like that moment to be – encased
in a bubble of warmth and love, uterine but the liquid now dried
into some kind of balmy ether, the heat of the washing machine
after its spin cycle. I remember, in that ambulance, diving head-
first into that bubble, into the void, like one of those Mexican
divers launching themselves off of daunting heights. I remember
travelling through the air in a way, less that was timeless, than
where time was irrelevant. It wasn't that I was soaring, not even
that I was floating, I was falling alright – and not like a feather, not
subject to the whim of gusts. I was a lead weight, dropping to the
bottom of a bottomless sea, a place that was sightless and smell-
less and tasteless and noiseless, where there was nothing to touch
– a place where all there was was falling, and where falling was an
ultimate goal, a glorious and final achievement. If my actual death
has one hundredth of the splendour of that swallow-dive, my
death will be splendid indeed. Glorious. I would not have been
able to dive as I did had my insides not been as clean as they were,
because of my earlier sobbing. Because of you.

Which brings us pretty much up to date. I'm now sitting in my
hospital bed, waiting for you and Saskja to arrive. I'm tired. It's
been quite a strain, getting all this written. The doctors have recom-
mended complete rest. They didn't want me even to write. So
going to Ulm's funeral ...! I know you know that. And I am very
grateful that you have chosen to act in accordance with my wishes
rather than the strictures of the doctors. "The strictures of the scriptures", remember? Remember that laugh of Ulm's?

I think he was bending forward to kiss me. I think it was a
prelude to seduction. I should like to have been Ulm's lover. I
suspect I would have been the only one. He'd have been, I think,
my first virgin. Though men do tend to lie, don't they, about such
things?

He got an erection after he died. I like to think that was courtesy
of me. I don't miss him. I don't miss any of them. Not any more.
Ulm, Arkona, my late and very unlamented husband, all the others
– friends, family, spiritual bedfellows ... and bed bedfellows. If I

miss anything, I miss in anticipation – of missing you, for instance, missing the sunrise in my bedroom, tsifalla and retsina and peanut butter sandwiches.

I will not wait here to die. I want to be at home. Want to see that sunrise as many times as I can before I die. That's not long away. I don't need to be told that's not long away. My body tells me that. Permanently. Oh, not in a threatening way: to reassure me.

Ah! Here you come. Late. What a surprise!

* * *

I'm back now in hospital. Back in bed. Well, I suppose that's obvious. It saddened me that they couldn't get my wheelchair up to the chapel for the burial, but I so totally agree that there could have been no other place to inter him.

I should also like to be laid to rest some place close to that, on our hill: Ulm's and mine, Arkona's and mine … yours and mine. You don't need to bury me there. By all means, burn me – if the Buddhists have not already eaten me! Maybe scatter my ashes – or my bones! – somewhere nearby. I'd like to think that was a soil which I could somehow mulch.

I have a need now to mulch too the soil which is you. I have a need to divest myself of … what is it? It's not knowledge. Knowledge is ubiquitous. There is nothing in the world easier to acquire than knowledge. And it's not wisdom. But it's the closest, I guess, I'll ever get to wisdom. It's the fruit of my labours. The farmer toils less for himself than for his successors – well, until recently, that is. I'd like to pass on the secrets of my orchard too before I shuffle onto orchards new. Death, I know, could claim me at any moment.

I am entirely ready to be claimed by death. This is no *grim* reaper, but a reaper of light and love and freedom, a reaper of orchards new and orchards unconfined, of treeless orchards where the fruit is the infinite air of breath, and breath is only a metaphor.

And if death claims me before I have ceded to you what I can, then that's alright. I can't supply your truth for you. The best I can hope is that some of my truth provides some kind of short cut to some of your truth.

The lie of any religion is that it *supplies* the truth. The best that any religion, any philosophy, can do is to supply this kind of short cut. They can tell you you have lungs, for instance, they can tell you what lungs do – the very best of them can even tell you where your lungs are – but the breathing you have to do for yourself.

Before I die, I'd like you to hear from me – I'd like Saskja also to hear – that you have lungs. Whether or not you use that information in order to breathe, that's your choice and your decision.

I know the conveyance we travelled in carries today some kind of ludicrously grandiloquent nomenclature, 'people carrier' or something absurd like that. To me it remains a minibus. You'd buried him, Ulm. The funeral was over. We were bumping over that pot-holed track that leads out of Marsalla. The stench of the slums still clung to the minibus, despite all the sweet-smelling chemicals they these days seem to infest the dashboard with. It was before the swanky pink house, whatever colour you'd call it. Not really pink, now I think about it – you know the one I mean – maybe a sort of plummy pink, a fuchsia sort of pink.

I was regretting having come at that stage, wishing I had been less headstrong, had listened more to medical opinion. You were both subdued, you and Saskja. She was confiding in you that at least the funeral had got her out of history. You were talking about how badly you'd been taught it, history.

"'Those who teach history," I said, "should remember the eighth Commandment."

"'Thou shalt not steal'?" you asked.

"If that Commandment had been obeyed," I said, "what a difference there would have been to world history. I wonder whether they'll ever teach you, Saskja, the fundamental of history: that the history of the world to date is the history of theft. Except that, because history is always written by the victors, we have called 'theft' 'conquest'.

"This is more lawyerese, a game of political semantics, and the result may well be the destruction of mankind.

"Even today 'generalship' is talked of as a virtue. What is 'generalship' except prowess in murder and in colossal theft, in causing grievous bodily harm, often to the totally innocent, in abetting rape and looting and pillage? Today we euphemise 'warfare' into 'defence'. What was 'defensive' about Alexander or Julius Caesar or Pizzaro? How can we continue to call any culture a 'civilisation', as we do the Roman, whose economy was dependent on enslaving fellow human beings, whose cruelty was indescribable, and whose 'entertainment' often involved gory and grizzly death? These, so our history books tell us, are mere peccadilloes against the triumphs of building straight roads and having houses with central heating!

"This interpretation of history doesn't, of course, make Hitler. But it contributes to the making of Hitler. It also contributes to the making of smaller monsters – so many of today's rulers, for example. Who are *that*: rulers. They seek to call themselves 'leaders', but if we allow ourselves to be led by them we will be led into the moral quagmire. We start becoming untrue to ourselves when we consider this type of ruler a 'leader'.

"And history itself must take a share of the blame for the fact that we don't learn from it. Man aspires to being god. And when he can't make god, he aspires to demi-godness. And we allow the odd man to become a demi-god. Alexander and Caesar are almost divine. Certainly they enjoyed a substantial 'life after death'. But living men too we install in the pantheon, and those that do nothing to deserve it – politicians who hanker for such status, screen stars, sportsmen, singers. They all love the laurels that we give them. Such adulation, though, also creates demi-demons. Because so many in the pantheon, latterday Neros, think their conduct is allowed to be outside that of mere mortals. And because the being in the pantheon is all that matters, the being remembered, the being someone who matters. It's that which gives you access to the pantheon. So many hoisted there arrive via ill deeds, via acts of cowardice. Whether you are considered a demi-god or a demi-demon matters very much less than the being remembered. You want to eradicate a yob society? Stop lionising yobs.

"The tragedy of history is that we have let it become 'the biographies of "great" people' – except that the biographied are those merely who have considered themselves 'great.' I feel sure that few who met them or had dealings with those 'great people' would agree with that description.

"If history started to be taught as the struggle of normal people to retain their integrity despite the crimes being perpetrated on them by those in power over them, far more people would be prepared to start owning their own integrity. We equate fame with greatness and greatness with worth – and that is a wholesale tragedy for mankind.

"Today the world's rulers are stealing our planet from us, they're stealing a future from our children, they're robbing most of the world of dignity and self-determination and, yes, integrity.

"A huge part of today's impoverished world is so because its resources were stolen by that part of the world now rich largely because of such theft. And then that rich world has the gall to consider what it pays back to these now impoverished countries 'loans' – not 'restitution', 'loans'. A burglar comes into your house, steals your television, then expects you to be grateful that he's prepared to rent your television back to you.

"There's a case being made by some Afro-Americans for back-pay earned by their slave forefathers. It is a debt which, if acknowledged, would bankrupt the U.S. Treasury. The debt owed by wealthy countries to Peru, for example, South Africa, India is likewise so enormous as to be unpayable.

"I don't say this to countenance lesser theft: The bloodied dictator robbing the coffers of international aid. Even the child dipping sticky fingers into his mother's purse is still stealing. It is an act which should, probably must, attract punishment. But, for God's sake – and I use that term advisedly – let us stop being so discretionary in our hearing of these Commandments.

"Let us condemn theft. Certainly. But let us condemn all theft. Business cartels are theft. Monopolies are theft. Business plundering natural resources is theft. Political corruption, nepotism, favouritism, protectionism – even inefficiency, all of this is theft. So is currency speculation, commodities brokering, and most of the dealings on the stock market. Banks foreclosing is often theft – Steinbeck shows us that.

"Theft is all around us. Mostly it is sanctioned. Often it is applauded. What is not forgiven is when the robbers are robbed from. And that is the rule of the Mafia.

"We are enjoined to look aghast at the Mafia. Yet what is the society in which we live but a rather larger, more complicated, often less honourable version of la cosa nostra? What distinguishes the protection-racketeer from the taxman? Or the banker? Except that the protection-racketeer extorts less money? What distinguishes the moral principles of a godfather and a president?

"If the rich countries, instead of basking in their cleverness and self-righteousness, started acknowledging their wealth as often being based on plunder, and started – not lecturing the impoverished world, not talking from atop a butter mountain of moral and economic superiority – but making proper restitution to it, paying back some of the loot stolen from it, the problems that will otherwise avalanche onto the twenty-first century will have taken a step in the right direction – away from being compounded and towards being solved. It would be a far bigger step for mankind than its walk on the moon.

"The impoverished of the world do not want Western money. They want *their* money back.

"And you know, such is the delinquent mentality today of the rich world, if the poor countries expressed it in those terms, the derisory trickle of money now flowing to them would probably stop. The West needs reparation to be seen as charity – charity with both a big and a small 'c', and demands at least gratitude in return.

"'… and the greatest of these is Charity'. I see a huge amount of charity at a personal level, one person to another. And at an official level, or at a corporate level, almost none.

"'Thou shalt not steal' – where does it end? Thou shalt not steal the air we breathe: by choking the atmosphere and hacking at the planet's lungs. Thou shalt not steal the planet's future: by allowing devastating weapons to proliferate, by failing to tackle the roots of crime, by failing to address the problems attendant on extreme poverty and on poverty extremely demeaning, or those of pandemics, global warming, over-population, over-farming, defor-estation, intellectual and cultural pollution. Thou shalt not steal dignity – by ensuring that I in a rich country need to keep people starving in order to keep my economy buoyant, or build weapons that warlords use to enslave, harry or terrify them.

"Is property theft? It's certainly the start of avarice. But is it theft? We each have to ask that of ourselves. And each has to answer it for him- or herself. Or, I suppose, not.

"In the same way that tennis players want their own racquets, I suspect early man may have wanted his own spear – the one that he had weighted to suit his throw, that had the grip on it he preferred. Is wanting such a spear theft? I read somewhere that, according to some zoologists, the acquisition of territory is the most powerful of all instincts – more powerful even than food or sex. And the acquisition of territory, by definition, means that others are deprived of it. When we deprive someone of something, is that immediately theft?

"Our six-year-old daughter paints us a picture at school, our son makes a model giraffe – these are our property. Priceless possessions, if we are wise. Is such property – such *treasure* – theft? Once we have two such pictures or two such models we have become acquisitive.

"We scour the beach for pretty shells or pebbles. We start to make a collection of such gems. We have become acquisitive.

"At what point does acquisition become theft?

"We allow legislation to decide that for us because it is so much easier than deciding it for ourselves. And now corporations hide behind such legislation. They even occasionally insist legislation be drafted.

"And me, I'm stealing time away from yours with Ezekiel, Giselle. I'm sorry."

"Don't be crazy, Lakshmi," you said. "Think I'd not have attended Ulm's funeral? You're *crazy*. Over and above which, your company, Lakshmi," you said, "your words, they're important to me. I have a voice. I can always say, 'Lakshmi, I'm going now.'"

"And you do know, don't you, you *can* always say that?"

"We're here," said Saskja. And they wheeled me back up to my room.

* * *

I know you'll be late. You always are.

And it's fine, Giselle. I'm not complaining, not even making a point. Just a moment of silliness, a feeble attempt at humour. It must be one of the greatest gifts in the world, being able to make people laugh. It's one I envy enormously.

I'm waiting. And it's entirely normal these days that I'm waiting. I seem to spend my entire day indeed waiting. I'm waiting for breakfast or for an injection or for a porter to arrive with my wheelchair. I'm waiting for a doctor or the results of a test or to be taken to the loo. I was always a doer. Even waiting, I used to do. Even standing in bus queues I was doing. And a lot of my doing, I see now, was doing so that I didn't need to think, was a think-substitute. Maybe that's where this is part of my destiny, maybe I need to be force-thought, like hunger-strikers are force-fed. But the worst of it is I'm not. Thinking. I've got into an attitude just of waiting. So, even when these days I am doing, I'm still waiting. Bathing, I'm waiting to dry myself, eating lunch I'm waiting for supper. It's pernicious. And I don't seem to be able to logic my way out of it.

God, it is so much harder to take advice than it is to give it. In my life I must have told scores of people, possibly hundreds, that logic has got nothing to do with feelings. So many people, I would tell them, are squeamish at the sight of blood. How logical is that? Blood is our life-source. We should be able to *bathe* in it, to wallow in it. Know what? Those who were squeamish at the sight of blood, following my advice, still were! Try to convince an arachnophobe through logic about the benefits of spiders.

We get angry at those who are dying. And then we feel guilty about our anger. "It's perfectly normal," I would tell those angry grievers, "to feel such anger. Those we love who are dying are causing us pain. We get angry with those who are causing us pain." And I'm right. I know I'm right. Even they know I'm right. But they still feel both the anger, and the guilt at feeling it. No amount of logicking is going to remove that from them.

And yet I still try to logic my way out of this, this attitude I seem to have adopted of waiting.

And it's not that I'm waiting to die. I've gone past that point. Death is, of course, very close. And I think we have more choice over it than we have over our birth – I'm not talking about suicide. I've heard from several nurses that, in the Casualty Department, they can spot which patients will live and which won't simply by the lustre in their eyes. Some burn with the determination to survive, others wilt in recognition that the fight has been extinguished.

My fight's gone, pretty much. I'm certainly not fighting death. Fighting life, maybe. Fighting for some kind of quality of life. I'm fighting presently so that I can get home again. I want to die at home. And that's yet another aspect of my life where logic plays no part.

I want to see the sunrise again. I'm waiting – and fighting – to see it. I can't see it from here. You've seen yourself. Even standing at the window there's almost no view. From my bed, I can see the eaves of that biliously yellow hotel opposite, a couple of straggly shards from the yucca tree, presumably on the next balcony, and 'that little patch of blue the prisoners call the sky'. Isn't that how Wilde described it? Something like that. Occasionally I see a sparrow as it descends onto the rail of my balcony, or sometimes a pigeon as it takes off from the yucca and flaps to get air-borne.

The sun I don't even feel till after lunch. Oh, it's quite light, this room, but scarcely sunny. I close my eyes each morning, in order to see and feel the sun rise. I see and feel it again as it is through my bedroom window. I feel chill slide like a trombone via no-chill and warmth to heat; I feel my skin stretching out to warmth and purring in the heat; I feel my insides shaking shivers off themselves like a dog emerging from the sea, feel them marshmallowing into glow and then splashing with the freedom of mountain rills just liberated from the bondage of being ice. I feel their joy, their tingle, their jubilation. And I feel the blood slinking round them like hot chocolate draped in mink, and I feel all those organs ah-ing in a surfeit of being cosseted and of knowing themselves pampered.

And I see each sun rise: I see the winter sun, twinkling through the frosted window-pane, its yellow pastel, its beam self-deprecating, apologetic, almost goofy; I see the vernal sun, a scarlet ball, cleft in two by a shard of jet-black cloud; I see it rise in summer, fiery, arrogant, dictatorial; and in autumn, swathed in a palette of the brightest hues, giant streaks of citric yellows and tangerine and the purples of plums, of damsons, of moonlit blueberries. But I want to see those sights not with my mind's eye, but with my head's eyes. However feeble those eyes might be.

If there is any fight in me, it's fight again to see that sunrise.

And to hear the birds trill to it, as their blood too slinks round their organs, and they are duveted with a non-exacting bonhomie.

You'll be here any minute. I'm still remarkably shy about these doodlings. I'm not quite sure why. Maybe, even those of us whose incapacity confiscates our privacy, we all have a need to retain – as well as dignity – some mystery. Maybe it's even that mystery which *is* that dignity – or at least vouchsafes it.

* * *

I'm tired now. You've just left, you and Saskja. It was quite a visit. And I find myself pulled in two directions at once: There is so much I want, and need, to commit to paper, and before I forget it; and I am exhausted. Emotionally, certainly, but physically too. Just wiped out. This pen feels in my hand the weight of a washing-machine. And about as unwieldy. Remember when we thought we'd save a fortune by plumbing it in ourselves? You were still Sóphia then, still in the convent. Not one of our better decisions.

Back to today … Barely had you crossed the threshold before you announced, "You were right, Lakshmi: God *is* an addict."

"Is this a new encyclical from the Pope?" I asked, rather wittily I thought given the time I had to think of it.

"It's her new pet theory," Saskja said. She entered the room some way behind you, laden with magazines … and grapes. "I tried to tell her she was better off with a cat, but … In fact, it is, her theory, quite like a papal encyclical – in so far as both are bull."

"Oh very good, Saskja," I exclaimed. And it really was, wasn't it? If, that is, it was as spontaneous as she would have liked us to believe!

"Not God the Father I'm talking about," you said. "God the Holy Ghost. It's the God the Holy Ghost Who's an addict. The God of a godless world."

"That's a relief," I said. "For one ghastly minute there, I thought you might be on the verge of blasphemy, but if it's only the Holy Ghost who's a junkie, why, I can't imagine that *anyone's* feathers would be ruffled by that."

You said, "You're very playful today."

To which I replied, "You know? I was rather hoping it might be you who was. That this idea of God the Holy Ghost being an addict was a bit of playfulness."

"Well, yes and no," you said. Saskja had plonked all the magazines down on that grey armchair. Now she went into the bathroom to wash the grapes. "I blame Ezekiel," she said, as she was going.

"Oh?" I asked of you.

"He took me to an NA meeting," you said. "That's Narcotics Anonymous, Lakshmi."

"And there I was, thinking I was old," I said. "Not realising I had only been born yesterday."

"So, you know, then, do you," you asked, not without testiness, "about the twelve steps, all that?"

"In another form, I've even studied them," I replied. Well, I like to think I replied. I may have smirked just a little too.

"Why?" you asked, suspiciously. Or was it enviously? Saskja returned from the bathroom, dropped the still wet fruit into the bowl which had only just been emptied of its previous offering. The bunch was too big for it, much of the fruit cascaded over its edge. The sunlight caught the water on the fruit and made it glisten. It was a beguiling sight.

"They enjoined me to ask some right questions of myself," I said. "Not all of us has a compulsion to escape, but there have certainly been times when I've wanted to. Even prolonged periods – three months, on one occasion. Only the foolish see a dentist exclusively when they have tooth-ache."

"You went to a meeting?" you asked.

"No," I replied. "No, I've never been to a meeting."

"I didn't, by the way, say the Holy Ghost is a junkie. Only that He's an addict."

"And that's a distinction, I'm sure, that the Spanish Inquisition will deem more than sufficient to keep you from the flames."

"I don't know what He's addicted to," you continued, ignoring me, other than with a quarter smile of acknowledgement that I had spoken. "I don't think it's junk. A junkie's addicted to junk."

"I get the point," I said. Saskja was looking at me, trying (I think) to gauge my reaction. I wonder what she saw. Even now, I'm not sure what my reaction was. Or is. I don't even know what my reaction is to not knowing what my reaction is.

"It came to me almost as an epiphany," you said, and your eyes were indeed gleaming as I imagine Paul's did on that famous Damascus road. I suspect always there is that gleam when first you gaze upon a naked truth – a lustful eye, an eye that wants to possess it and ravish it. It doesn't matter whether that truth has a wider application than to you. All that matters, at that moment, is that this is your truth. And your truth has chosen to expose itself to you, and to allow you to see it in all its varicose veins and wrinkles and layers of fat – in all the imperfections of its perfection.

"The God, Lakshmi," you continued, "as I said before, of a godless world." I looked from you to Saskja.

"Don't look at me," she said. "I've heard all this before."

"The dynamo that runs the world, it has the spirit of an addict," you said. "All our talk of the ten Commandments ..."

"We've only got to nine," I reminded you.

"When I went to the meeting," you said, "we'd only then got to eight." You were gazing out of the window, but were immersed in the view inside yourself. You didn't want to look at us – either Saskja or me. That quarter-smile you'd given was a flick in my direction, nothing more. "That doesn't matter. What does is that, suddenly, all of it, it made sense.

"It's your analogy, Lakshmi, not mine – if analogy is the right expression: that the dynamo of the world, the *moral* dynamo, is the Holy Ghost. All I'm saying is, *if* your analogy holds water, then that Holy Ghost is an addict. The world's moral dynamo at the moment is an addict."

"Go on," I said to you, with a similar hesitation to yours when I had first mooted that analogy.

"An addict," you said, "is someone incapable of dealing with reality, opting rather for fantasy."

I looked again at Saskja. "Oh yes," she said, "there *is some* truth in it." I think she holds some kind of torch for you, Giselle. Intellectual torch, I'm talking about. She squeezed that observation into a pause you'd taken just to restock your lungs.

"An addict never grows up. The fix is the only thing important to him. He'll sell the family silver – even the family – to get it. Lying is second nature to him – and becomes anyway distorted by the confusion in his head between reality and fantasy. He wants, in Bob Dylan's phrase, to 'forget about today until tomorrow'. That's on the one hand: the *repercussions* he wants tomorrow – but the tomorrow in which he wants those repercussions is that tomorrow which never comes. The gratification, on the other hand, he wants *now*. Not even today. *Right* now, right this instant. The addict has no room in his life for God. Mostly because he thinks he *is* God – or, at the very least, that the universe revolves around him and his needs. This combines with a very deep self-loathing, which leads to masochism, self-harming, self-mutilation, even suicide.

"In what regard, Lakshmi, does that world out there, the world today, differ from that picture of an addict?"

"Does it help?" I asked. "Even if the depiction is accurate, isn't it all rather defeatist? I mean, if the Holy Ghost is an addict, and if the end of an addict is often suicide, does it help us to know that? Supposing it's true, does the analysis help?"

You did turn round at that point, and you gave out a sort of strangulated laugh of disbelief. "We're in a hospital, Lakshmi," you said.

"Amazing, Holmes," I said. "However do you do it?"

"You know how many illnesses and conditions are being treated here?" you asked.

"Go on," I returned. "Amaze me."

"I have no idea," you said, with a more genuine smile. "But one thing I do know, all those conditions – the thousands of them, I suppose there are – they've all got one thing in common: They cannot start to be treated until they have been diagnosed."

"It's a fair point," Saskja commented.

"You know the biggest problem with treating any addiction?" you asked. Before I could reply, you answered your own question, "Denial," you said. "The problem of persuading an addict he is one, the problem of persuading him there *is* a problem."

"Alright," I said. "It is a fair point you're making, Giselle. I do concede that."

"I never hear talk about the problem being suffered by the moral dynamo of the world, of the Holy Ghost's problem," you said. "I hear plenty about climate change, and ecological damage. I hear about species on the verge of extinction, and of genocides, and

of acute poverty and pandemics. I hear about lawlessness and
violence and it not being safe to walk on the streets. I hear about
the bombing of New York and Baghdad. But I rarely hear that there
might be a sickness underpinning all this – and if I do hear about
it, I hear about it from some bastion of the Church, trying to
support a no longer supportable institution. Or premise. It is the
sickness that needs to be addressed, Lakshmi: the illness itself, not
the symptoms.

"Once the illness starts to be treated, the symptoms will,
inevitably and of themselves, start to erode and then to disappear."

"'Thou shalt not bear false witness against thy neighbour'?" I
suggested.

"You think this is bearing false witness against the Holy
Ghost?" you asked, almost indignantly. I wanted to interrupt then,
but you were clearly expecting antagonism and pushed on, like an
old-fashioned steam train, gathering speed, gathering momentum.
"You know, Ezekiel's ex-girlfriend, she told him he had a dope
problem. And he called her every name under the sun. Eventually
she gave him an ultimatum, either you seek treatment or I go. At
the time he was resentful beyond measure. Today he recognises it
as one of the greatest acts of love that has been shown him. Don't
look at me like that, Lakshmi," you scowled. "He's not still with
her. I wish he were, actually. It'd get me out of a hole."

I let that pass, but I noticed Saskja raise the kind of eyebrow
which indicated she'd be talking to you about that on your way
home.

"It's the ninth Commandment," I reminded you. "If we are
going to base treatment on diagnosis," I went on, possibly a mite
crankily, "do you not think it important that we examine the
patient thoroughly?"

"I think it's essential," you said. I think you wanted me more
readily to accept your diagnosis, and to applaud you for it. I
suspect Saskja had, and that her sarcasm when you had both
arrived (if indeed 'sarcasm' was what it was) was voiced to desac-
charine her earlier plaudits. And, Heavens, I do understand your

disappointment – with my lack of applause, I mean. But sometimes the highest compliment of all is an apparent nothing. Ask a diva. The ovation most they cherish is one, as the curtain falls, when there is silence. For a long breath. And *then* the ovation begins. Well, I don't know that I was in exactly that situation, to be frank, but your words were not those I could simply admire. They needed – and need – to be thought about. I still have to think about them. And that's the highest praise that can be afforded any theory, to any thesis too or theorem: that it be considered.

You came to sit on the edge of the bed. You spied the grapes as we were talking. To begin with, they were just there, in your field-of-vision. And then – and I could see it – they became within your field-of-action. Eventually, and almost defiantly, you leant forward and took a grape. Then you took another. And another. Finally, your eyes still on me, still defying me to forbid you or to challenge you, you took the whole bowl, and (cradling it rather as you had me on the bathroom floor) set about eating your way through the whole bunch. It reminded me so much of when you had determined to avenge yourself on your Mother Superior by taking a lover. This was a permanent sub-text, over which we said:

"Lying has so many forms, perjury likewise, slander … so many forms." That was me.

"We, most of us," I went on, "know the fault – and faults – of language. Yet so few of us make any allowance for it. You're looking lost, Saskja."

"I don't think I'm most of us:" she said, with that disarming candour of hers. "I don't know the fault of language."

"It's a very inexact form of communication," I told her. "The talker can only ever be as good as the listener. Not even Shakespeare can speak to those who will not hear him. Even with the best will existing between the two protagonists there are, in any exchange, three separate elements, often mutually exclusive: There is what I mean to say, what I do say and what is heard.

"It's the basis of so much comedy. And we watch that comedy, and we laugh at it, but …"

"We're lousy learners?" you suggested.

"Lousy. Amongst their many other faults, schools (at least, the schools I went to) seem to suggest that only in an academic situation can we learn, preferably whilst being bored senseless. It's such a travesty. Great comedy, for instance, is often also greatly educational – it teaches us about our foibles, our weaknesses, it keeps us right-sized." Saskya nodded sagely. But she was doing so to impress you. That was about the time you started nibbling at the grapes.

"Power," I said, "only comes in two flavours: oppression or persuasion. As an institution, government vastly prefers the former. It makes its life so very much easier. And for that reason we must always – *always* – be on our guard whenever government moves in the direction of oppression. Who was it said, 'The price of freedom is constant vigilance'?"

"Sorry," you admitted.

"I can't remember either," I confessed.

"What was that again?" Saskja asked. You repeated it.

"We would all do well to remember that adage," I said, "even if we can't remember its author. It is an adage with a dreadful pertinence to our times."

You munched on yet another grape, and said, "I do remember it was Burke who said, 'All that is needed for evil to succeed is for good men to do nothing.' *Edmund* Burke, that is."

"Another adage worth the remembering. Even when, as today, good men are increasingly disabled from doing anything. And that too is a part of 'Thou shalt not bear false witness against thy neighbour'."

"Disabled?"

"Censorship is disablement. And censorship *is* censorship even if it's by debarring entry to the popular media. The fact is that the public is continuously being lied to. Oh, the magnates and the politicians will point to tiny outlets and insist, were censorship in operation, such outlets would not be allowed to exist. But we have moved on from the KGB and Goebbels. Those in power cannot any longer be *seen* to be censoring thought. So they restrict thought to those areas where they think it will do least damage – to those outlets, in other words, where their critics would inevitably anyway be skulking. Keep it away from areas where new critics could be recruited.

"It is so ominous, the restrictions being placed on free thought by the need, in the words of Western governments, to combat the 'War on Terror'. We must be grateful for the resilience, and sometimes the subterfuge, of truth. It usually worms its way through the tightest control. Because, finally, it has to.

"It's more pernicious, this control," I said, "than just the coverage of politics, international politics or war or economics. Even in crime shows – cops-and-robbers stuff – the crooks are now invariably thugs, with no redeeming qualities at all. And the cops, whilst 'human' and thus frail, are entirely justified in referring to such people as 'pond life' and treating them accordingly. Murdering an escaping felon is an act of courage, even of patriotism. Those lawyers who defend such law-breakers are only one step removed from pond-life, ambulance-chasers whose only interest is in making as many dishonest bucks as they can.

"This is all bearing false witness against our neighbours.

"Lying by exclusion has become a norm. So has lying by journalese. How to paint a bloated capitalist … 'Birds,' the article reads, 'sing in the tree-lined crescent, a Rolls-Royce Corniche stands outside the door …' The 'tree-lined crescent' is a dirt track cul-de-sac with a couple of straggly bushes either side of it, the Rolls-Royce has been hired by the reporter. 'Questions have been asked about Mr X's past'. Asking Mr X where he went to school is to raise a question about his past. All such ruses too are bearing false witness.

"Deliberately distorting someone's words, there is another. And how often is that used as a ruse? In debate? In journalism? Which returns us to power by persuasion.

"'Thou shalt not bear false witness' is contrary to governmental, even political, policy. Government by oppression bears false witness by exclusion. Indeed you can say that any government which deliberately fails to let its citizens know the whole truth of a situation is an oppressive government, and one that has to become an oligarchy. How many oppressive governments, by that definition, how many oligarchies are there in the world today?

"But government by persuasion is also one which bears false witness. Over centuries the system has grown of adversarial politics, of politics by confrontation, by advocacy. In which a large element is the destruction of your opponent's argument. In order to accomplish which, that argument is frequently distorted into a parody of itself. It is a tactic of the debater and of the lawyer. Perhaps it is inevitable. But it is nevertheless in direct contravention of this Commandment. And probably the world is the poorer place for that contravention.

"I say 'probably' because there are things which are incomprehensible to me. If the primary job of government is to protect its citizens, how can there be any question about providing those citizens with free health care? The best that is available? How is attack by virus less sinister or life-threatening than that by human invaders? How do countries, on the one hand, imprison those who sexually molest its children, but honour those who refuse those children medical treatment? Or *sufficient* medical treatment? Or allow them to be malnourished?

"How can any state which claims to protect its citizens not be devoting money to education sufficient to the task? Most children today, even in the richest countries, are not even schooled well, and the idea of education seems to be an ancient and quaint anachronism.

"We seem to be sliding into a barbarism of hi-tech lethargy, one where virtual life is more important than real life, where virtual human rights are a reasonable ersatz and where virtual democracy, virtual responsibility, virtual accountability are considered good enough. And there are those in the representational bodies of what they would like to consider 'civilised' countries who use extensive rhetorical skills to defend such positions, even to advocate them as being proper."

"How do you know, though, if something is proper?" Saskja asked.

"You simply ask yourself, are people being hurt by this," I suggested to her. "By a lack of health care, by inadequate schooling, we are *all* being hurt. Badly in today. And in tomorrow devastatingly. And all those who seek to tell you otherwise are bearing false witness not only against their neighbour and neighbours, but against the totality of humanity."

"Doesn't this just prove my point?" you asked "That the Holy Ghost is an addict?"

* * *

"Talk about the last Commandment," Saskja commanded me.

"Why don't *you* tell *me* about it?" I suggested. "I'm fairly talked out. Or Giselle, maybe?"

"'Thou shalt not covet thy neighbour's wife'?" you said.

"If I remember rightly," I replied, "it's also anything 'belonging' to thy neighbour." This was when you replaced the bowl on the bedside table. There were about four grapes left!

"Well," you said, "'not coveting his wife', that would be Hollywood out of the window."

"Right," I said.

"Quite a lot of the pizzazz in politics," Saskja added.

"A lot of it, quite."

"But ..."

"Yes?" I asked.

"When," you asked, "does coveting start?"

"Ah!" I said.

"I mean, where does attraction end and coveting start?"

"A good question indeed. There's another good question being begged too by this Commandment."

"There is?" you asked again.

"How would the neighbour's wife feel about not being

coveted?"

"It's a male charter again, isn't it?" Saskja suggested.

"Is it?"

"If the woman isn't coveted," Saska continued, "the man really doesn't need to do much within the relationship."

"Just as sinisterly," it was my turn to suggest, "it implies that we can control our emotions. And we can't. We can control the actions occasioned by those emotions. But all we can do with the emotions themselves is either to deny them, which is extremely unhealthy, or own them. If we own them they have less power over us than if we deny, and therefore suppress, them."

"So, it's a what, then? A stupid Commandment, this one?" you asked. "An unenforceable one?"

"It's certainly unenforceable. It's also ill-advised. It feeds the shame that the Church used for so long to control us. The Catholic Church even goes so far as to insist that we 'confess' our 'impure "thoughts"' – as if our instincts were things we could control, and therefore that we need feel guilty about. We have absolutely no control over those we find attractive. We only have control over what we do about it. We have no control either over liking strawberries or disliking beetroot, over the pain of a broken leg or a broken heart, over that which tickles us or ticks us off. We only – again – have control over what we do about such stimuli.

"Do you think, rather than a Commandment forbidding us to covet our neighbour's ... let's say 'spouse' ..."

"Let's say 'partner'," you suggested.

"Rather than that, the enjoinment might not have read better to do nothing to impair or compromise the integrity of that person – that spouse, partner, whatever? By, I don't know, demeaning him or her, for example? Or humiliating, deriding, mocking, belittling him or her?"

"You think that would have stopped it? Such abuse?" Saskja asked.

"I think it might have enjoyed more success than not coveting."

"Does the same apply, then, to the rest of the Commandment?"

you asked.

"If we all obeyed the material side of the tenth Commandment, Giselle," I replied, "the world's economy would collapse. The economy as we have allowed it to become today, the economy of the crib. It's no longer that governments *want* to laud greed and applaud usury. Their wishes are not any longer of the slightest concern. It's that they *have* to.

"As in so many things, they are the Frankenstein who has created a monster now no longer under his control."

"'Thou shalt not covet thy neighbour's belongings.' Milton Friedman would be horrified. Monetarism is the economic regression into infancy. It validates selfishness, grants respectability to greed. It's not about free markets or free trading, it's about giving free rein to bullies. Those who claim to espouse monetarism as an altruistic belief are the Pharisees of economics. They no more believe in free markets than industrialists believe in capitalism. How much freedom is there in the computer market? Does the cartel still exist which regulates the price of soap powder? And perfumes? What collusion exists between the High Street banks?

"I have heard European film actors eulogising the United States because there success is not envied. I have little idea what they mean by that. I suspect rather too many believe their own demi-god status and are insulted when Europeans fail to venerate, or even adore, them in the manner they have come to consider their due. But to claim of the United States that it is a society without envy is to claim that the Amazon lacks water. It is a claim which completely flies in the face of the evidence.

"American – and thus, increasingly, global – culture is *founded* on envy. And, principally, envy of the material. Because now generations of those of us in the West have fallen for that insane belief that material comfort will lead to emotional comfort. And that, of course, doesn't mean (as those who seek to bear false witness would have you believe it means) that material comfort is not important. To tell someone who is starving that money won't make them happy is ... grotesque. Billie Holliday probably summed it all up, 'I've been rich,' she said, 'and I've been poor. Being rich is better.' Of course it is. The mistake is not in wanting material comfort, but in thinking that such is the *source* of emotional or psychological or spiritual well-being.

"Ever since Freud's nephew, Edward Bernays, started applying his uncle's tenets to the job of advertising, the acquisition of goods has stopped being about the acquisition of goods. It hasn't been about the television set itself or the cigarette or the car. It has become a way of measuring our success, and thus our value; it has been a romantic or sexual lure; it has been about validation. Of course, what so few men have yet to realise is that the only woman lured by a Ferrari is a woman who is lured by a Ferrari. But, then, that's men!

"Globalisation depends on us all envying those with Ferraris and plasma screen televisions and electronically operated gates – whatever new toy is for the manufacturers the most lucrative. Very few of us will get to do anything but gape through the bars of our playpen at such extravagant gewgaws, but it's important – it's *vital* – that we should all covet them.

"And we need to borrow in order to buy the pale imitations of such trinketry. Because borrowing keeps us compliant, it concentrates our mind only on the debt, there is no space left for questions or complaint.

"Gone – or, at least, going – are the days when we worked to live. Globalisation exacts the price that we live only to work. Pausing only long enough to get ourselves further into debt by buying the latest essential on the market – the interest on which debt ensures that we have to work even longer hours. And all these essentials (with governmental sanction) are manufactured with a built-in expiry date, so that further outlays will be occasioned every couple of years to ensure we all *remain* in debt.

"This is not only the economics of the crib, but of the Christmas tree when we were in that crib: all the parcels glittering beneath the tinsel and the flashing lights – a second or two of joy and a whole lot of disappointment when the paper is shredded and the ribbons cut.

"Young people, so I've been told, lack the time for courtship. Relationships aren't allowed to burgeon or develop in their own time. If there isn't an immediate prospect of permanency, the two individuals concerned move smartly onto the next. Frankly, I fail to see *how* any relationship can be built on such a foundation. But, assuming it can, if lovers don't have time for each other, what hope is there that, should those lovers become parents, those parents will have any time for their children? Deprive a generation of time and you will have sired a generation that is extremely troubled. At precisely the time that the planet needs a generation with incredible ease, robust health and remarkable insight. Needs such a generation as a matter of survival."

"You're pricking my conscience," you said.

"Ezekiel?"

"I think I'd better go." You started getting your things together, nodded to Saskja that she should do likewise. She was in some kind of reverie. She suddenly saw what you were doing, and stood up, collecting her various bits around her.

"You know," I said, "there's something really quite curious about the ten Commandments."

"Curious?" Saska asked.

"We're forever being encouraged, aren't we?, to be positive, to think positively: If life hands us lemons, we're to make lemonade, all that sort of worthy advice."

"And?"

"Eighty per cent of the Commandments are negative. Where are the seven lively virtues? How much of our much-pilloried negativity has been fed to us by Churches eager to control us?"

"Good," said Saskja unenthusiastically. "Yet something else to think about."

With which, and a few courtesies, and "look after yourself"s, you both went.

* * *

There *is* one thing more, though. Something I was thinking about when you were here, but which has only really just formed myself properly in my brain. Something else I'd urge you both to think about. At some time. I think it might help you.

Some time ago, I mentioned a theory, that all the Commandments are, in fact, variations on the theme of 'Unto thine own self be true'. Let's just travel with that theory for a moment. And let's also express the Commandments as positive, and not negative, exhortations. Would this, do you think, be a fair paraphrase of those Commandments? One, maybe, with greater application, greater relevance to today?

First Commandment: Respect your integrity, your principles.

Number Two: Respect the integrity and principles of others.

Three: Respect the critics of those principles – but only if those critics themselves have principles.

Four: Respect the time you need to review and, if necessary, adjust those principles.

Five: Respect your past and your future so that your present may be whole.

Six: Respect the physical lives of those around you – and your own.

Seven: Respect the *private* lives of those around you – and your own. Respect their dignity and yours.

Eight: Respect the *material* lives of those around you – and your own.

Nine: Respect your own honesty.

Ten: Respect what are genuinely your own best interests – which, if you *are* genuine, have also to be the best interests of others.

As I said, just something for you to think about.

* * *

Oh, the relief. To be home again. To be surrounded by all the mess and the junk that is me. And probably, as much as anything, defines me. We can't help the gifts we are given, of course – the knick-knacks and the bric-à-brac of far too many birthdays –, but what we keep goes some way to defining us. What prominence we give what pieces.

A friend of mine, a writer, his office is crammed with all his 'completely favourite' books – as opposed to the merely 'favourite' books of his which he has lining every other wall in his tiny flat. The souls of writers, he maintains, are contained within their books. He likes to think of those souls lightly nudging his pen, sprinkling their fairy-dust on the paper.

And I suppose that beliefs, I don't know, like Feng Sh'ui, maybe, work in a similar way. If the colour red stands for money, in other words, any time you see something red you will think of money. And it is that concentration, that permanent reminder of it, it is that which leads you to the making of it. In a way not dissimilar to the way Ulm – God bless him – described prayer: Its power is not in the metaphysical so much as the physical seeking contact with the metaphysical. It is the cerebral acknowledging the cerebral is not enough. It is the immense power of powerlessness.

You've gone home to pack. God bless you, Giselle. I cannot begin to express my gratitude. I would be very nervous living alone in this place. '*Even* in this place,' maybe I should write. To be frank, I'm quite nervous at the moment. I keep imagining every crack I hear is the start of a fire, every creak in this wheelchair is signalling its imminent collapse. There is as well the absolute *powerlessness* of powerlessness!

I'm just not going to think of that. I'm basking in what I like to think of as 'my' light here – the flat's light, the quality of light that is peculiar to it. And its warmth too. There is a 'warm' I feel here that I have felt nowhere else on the planet. Not true: Sometimes also on 'our' hillside. Occasionally there. As if God had designated to a particular thermal Lakshmi's 'warm', or something. It's the warm ... well, of warmth itself, of course. But liberally seasoned with gemütlichkeit and peace and okayness and unthreateningness and not-having-to-put-on-an-actness, whatever the word is – contrivance, I suppose. Yes, very liberally seasoned with a lack of contrivance. This is where my soul fills its pipe and dons its slippers.

As well as no 'place', there is also no smell like home. Oh, you notice it particularly having returned from a place where the smells are mostly chemical – of disinfectant and aerosoled 'air-freshener' and starch and furniture polish. Strong smells designed presumably to expunge the pongs of vomit, shit and blood. It's more of the twenty-first century: disguising the real with the synthetic. I'm not wild about the smell of any excretions, but they are not allayed by other substances far more toxic than they are. All you do is to get the smell of excretions *and* excrescences.

Do you know, I don't know *what* this place smells of? I've been trying to analyse it as I write. Home, I suppose, finally. It smells of home. The whole smell, it's permeated with Lakshmi: my clothes smell of me and the washing powder which *I* bought, which *I* prefer, which *I* used to wash them with. The kitchen is imbued with the smells of the foods I like to cook – and to eat. This sitting room ... there's the smell of the woollen tapestry, of the leather pouffe, of the oranges which have gone off since I was in hospital and which I'm going to throw away as soon as I've finished this but which, for all their offness, still smell delicious. There's the smell of the books and that of the television, of the Orphalese dust (a fair amount of that!), and the hangover of the polish I used the last time I cleaned. It's a cumulative smell, and it smells home and it smells familiar. It finally smells, as I said, Lakshmi.

I'm avoiding the issue. Really, I'm sure when you return we'll talk about it again. How could we not?

I was surprised, to be frank. Maybe I was even shocked. That shock was probably more to do with me, than you. And I suppose there was a part of me shocked that I was shocked. Shocked with myself. And not a little aghast *at* myself. Shocked that my first reaction was to be so judgemental. I've made a study, so I like to think, of non-judgementalism. Even of individual politicians, even of so-called celebrities whose views can anthrax continents, I tried not to judge the person, just the opinion, just the policy.

My first thought, though, was: You're cheating on Ezekiel. 'Cheating', where did that concept come from? As if a relationship were a game of cards, or something. That's already judgemental. And it's a phrase we use in everyday conversation. Such, of course, underscores its judgementalism. Monogamy is not innate in us – we've established that. It is a choice. And it is the right of any couple to make that choice: the right of both the people which constitute that couple, of course. 'Being unfaithful', that's another judgemental phrase. If you have made the vow 'forsaking all others', then you have been unfaithful to that vow. That much is true. You haven't, though (at any rate, as far as I know), made that vow.

And there is that problem with theories – or whatever else it is you like to call them: That's what they are. They're theories. And thus likely to be disproved by events – or not be up to the case in point, or fall short of the entire picture, or ... or ... or. And the problem with principles is similar.

To be at my most charitable, and at its best, this age could be called the Age of Empiricism – an age where only experience counts, of the practical and pragmatic as opposed to the philosophic and idealistic, of realpolitik usurping the quest for Utopia. That Age would seem to suggest that, whatever the principle, because we are humans, we are inevitably going to fall short of it. And therefore, knowing that we are going to fail, or fall short, there is no point even aiming for it.

Which, of course, is a philosophy in itself. Albeit one of convenience. And like most 'convenient' things, convenience is almost its only virtue. Just as citrus flavouring can only suggest the actual taste of an orange (which continue to waft mouth-wateringly over me as I write), so a convenience truth or a synthetic truth or an ersatz truth can only hint at the variety and depth of both taste and texture contained in real truth.

Real truth is unattainable. Maybe even by God. But in stopping to seek for it, in stopping our 'quest' for it, we let in the lie. And the lie is like the crab-grass outside my window: It spreads voraciously, and is very difficult to get rid of. Principles too are defined, not by themselves, but by our striving towards them.

People have principles. Most people have very strong principles. Governments do not. Nor do institutions. Or, more accurately, the principles of government have always been expendable commodities. And we are today paying the price for that. Governments are like children (in so many ways!): very specific parameters have to be laid down within which they have to operate. Yet another reason why government loves wars is that, in times of war, 'national security' demands a culture of covertness. Behind which same cloak can be hidden an entire motley of other secrets – gaffes, at its best and, at its worst, crimes.

Principles today are seen to stand in the way of what pundits like to call 'progress'. And never does anyone nail their feet to the floor for long enough to know how such vaunters of 'progress' define it. There are few definitions of 'progress' which would apply to the world today.

Except for that of the people themselves. Do people care more today? Not for their local community, that much is true. But then architects, at the government's request, made sure there wasn't too much local community. Local community was fostering too much discontent. But people do today have more care for global and international matters. Despite the barrage of propaganda – in the newspapers they read, in television, in advertisements, in advertorials, in the programmes and articles, on the back of cereal packets, bus tickets, in statements from the bank, the building society or the Post Office, despite all these billions of bacterial sound-bytes and sight-bytes, people do care. Enormously. And globally.

They care for the wider world and (despite the best endeavours of the plutocrats) know more about it; they care more about global issues; they are becoming more aware of themselves and what it means to take responsibility for themselves. And the plutocrats are terrified of that consciousness and that conscience.

The plutocrats, to guard their kingdoms, are perfectly prepared to sacrifice the rest of the planet. 'Better dead than red' also applies to you. In other words, the adherents to such a policy (or any other political hue you may choose to name) are not only prepared to die themselves, they're also more than perfectly prepared that you should also die.

In fact, most of those plutocrats would enormously prefer that you did the dying on their behalf. How many of today's politicians in areas with armed forces in the field have children serving with the military?

And whether or not you agree with the axioms whereby the plutocrats live their lives has nothing to do with their preparedness that you should die. And that your children should die – even if they are too young to have an opinion.

And your children's children, and your children's children's children, even unto the umpteenth generation.

And that the three billion people there are on this Earth too poor to have an opinion, that they should die alongside us all.

This is a tyranny, in scale, without parallel. That it is a tyranny rarely perceived as being such is only an indication of just how virulent and stubborn has been the spread of the crab-grass lie. It's a tyranny which, at least domestically, prefers a subtle oppression. It is no less oppressive for its subtlety.

Scruples are, of course, the luxuries of the well-heeled. To tell someone who is starving that it is against a Commandment that they should scrump windfall apples, that such is theft, indicates the unscrupulousness not of the scrumper but of his castigator. (Such 'theft' was also, I understand, excluded from the original understanding of 'Thou shalt not steal'. 'Thou shalt not steal' never, in Biblical times, meant that the poor should starve. This was an understanding of two thousand years ago! How was it, again, that we defined 'progress'?)

But scruples are not principles. Even societies which are starving create principles, even totally immoral or amoral societies

– American prison yards, for instance – have a code of ethics, however warped.

There is a problem in the world today with personal morality – and the line increasingly becomes blurred between the amoral and the immoral. How could there not be a problem when we are all surrounded by the immoral and the amoral?

But the biggest problem we have with morality is not with personal morality, not even with the violent gangs prowling the street, or organised crime, it is the amorality and/or immorality at institutional and governmental levels. Government today – just as, historically, the Church – is enjoining its subjects to abide by a code of standards which it spectacularly does not live by itself.

And in that, it not only countenances the lack of morality required by business, it encourages it. It has to encourage it. When we hear a senior politician lambaste the 'yob culture' his policies have created, we have a classic example of the pimp censuring the whore. Not even that: it is a classic example of the unapologetic father, censuring his daughter for prostituting herself when it is he who has put her on the streets.

I suppose I'm happy for you. You say you love Rodolfo, that your affair with Ezekiel was only a fling, an entrée to the entrée of a romantic attachment coupled (if that's not too unfortunate a word) with sexual attachment – that which you have with Rodolfo. I worry that you will be hurt. But then I would also worry were you to live without hurt. It is not the only thing that deepens us, but it is an essential part of the mix.

'No pain no gain' has always struck me as a masochist's charter. Not that I have anything against masochists, except if their predilection accompanies a claim to the moral high ground. I do not consider the zealots of Opus Dei who daily attach garters of hooks to their thighs are any more holy than the garterless firemen rushing to a burning building.

Certainly pain seems to be endemic to the maturing process: teething is painful, childhood very painful, puberty (at least for me) agonizing. Maybe not *all* gain is therefore possible without pain, but certainly some is. Many other things, for instance, may deepen us. Things that are pleasurable. Appreciation, say, of good food or good art, the joy of good conversation and companionship, the delight of parenthood (as well as its many woes) – the ecstasy, Giselle, of passion. All these can be our teachers. And, if we are wise, we grow with each new experience.

Of course Nietzsche was right with his famous adage, 'That which does not kill us makes us stronger', but that doesn't mean, in order to attain strength, we have to constantly put ourselves in life-threatening situations. A cake may need flour as a basic ingredient. Try baking a cake with flour alone.

We're taught at school that learning is a dull undertaking, an academic 'discipline', as they call it. Also in school 'discipline' is used as a synonym for 'punishment'. Small surprise then that schoolchildren shy away from 'discipline' like wax before a flame. 'Discipline', though – *properly* administered and looked after – is, in fact, not limiting at all, it is incredibly liberating. Brushing your teeth regularly is a discipline. It makes your mouth feel good, it makes you hugely nicer to talk to and (especially) to kiss, and it saves the agony of tooth-ache. If we are wise, we don't even think about brushing our teeth. The event happens in the haze of habit. The more we surround ourselves with such good habits, the more time we have to question those habits whose worth is more ... questionable. Swearing an oath of allegiance, for instance, to a country currently acting illegally.

So, I both worry about you getting hurt and try to tell myself, at the same time, not to. I suppose I worry that you're selling yourself short. Or that Rodolfo is spinning you a line. Or that you've become entranced by sex itself ... all worries which have – you have no need to say it – nothing whatever to do with me.

My chariot swings low all of a sudden. Swings very low. It *is* a sweet chariot. It is wheel-less, pulled by Pegasus, its gondola swathed in swan's feathers, its inside nestled with their down. And it sings to me as it swings, sings sweetly to me as it swings ... as it swings lower ... lower still.

Thomas Aquinas deliberately left the book he was writing unfinished. He could have had a point. I fear I may have said too many things, fear lest I have articulated things better left unsaid. And yet I know I have indeed left many things unsaid. I know this book too is not yet finished.

Not finished, and yet complete. In a way I can't define – and that probably cannot be defined.

As I am. Complete. And fulfilled. And expended.

It's time now to cap the pen, and stopper the ink, to blot the final page. A page I can now barely see. What the scrawl must be like which spiders across that page … well, I just shudder to think.

Ever lower swings my chariot. Ever more sweetly does it sing to me.

My eyes stay open, but my seeing closes. It's like in the theatre: a slow fade to black. But it is a black alive with phosphorescent colour and bursting with fizzing light.

Giselle – Saskja, too, if you ever read this – indeed anyone who happens to light upon these pages, I now have to go. I leave you with Arkona's invocation:

"Citizens of Orphalese," he said, "I ask God to bless you. Please remember too to bless yourselves."

BOOKS

O books
O is a symbol of the world, of oneness and unity. In
different cultures it also means the "eye", symbolizing
knowledge and insight, and in Old English it means "place
of love or home". O books explores the many paths of
understanding which different traditions have developed
down the ages, particularly those today that express
respect for the planet and all of life.

For more information on the full list of over 300 titles
please visit our website
www.O-books.net

Prophet of the New Millennium
Gregory Dark

Few can address the issues of religion, politics, emotional confusion, sex and addiction; as articulately as Gregory Dark; yet never fully pontificate. Dark is redolent; neither over prescriptive nor judgemental. Extremely insightful, he clearly believes, that whatever your concept of God, the fact is, this entity is most of all present within. His point; we have lost contact with our inner selves; and with it, TRUTH and principles for the world. We can empower ourselves, and reclaim this ability and write a book of principles for an unprincipled age - with or without established religion. Dark presents this as a reality and exposes the culprits who have cast a veil over it. **Miriam O'Gara**, BA (Hons), DipLit. Lecturer in Classics
1905047576 128pp **£9.99 $16.95**

Deep Equality
Living in the Flow of Natural Rhythms
Jocelyn Chaplin

For many years, Jocelyn Chaplin has worked at the cutting edge of therapy, politics and conscious living. In this book she pulls together all the marvelous ideas and intuitions we have been hearing and experiencing at conferences and workshops. This is a text that academics, activists and anyone involved with the future of humanity should read, allowing themselves to become inspired by what Chaplin means when she writes of Deep Equality. **Andrew Samuels**, Professor of Analytical Psychology, University of Essex
9781846940965 160pp **£9.99 $22.95**

Love, Healing and Happiness
Spiritual wisdom for secular times
Larry Culliford

This will become a classic book on spirituality...immensely practical and grounded. A nourishing book that lays the foundation for a higher understanding of human suffering and hope. **Reinhard Kowalski,** Consultant Clinical Psychologist and author of *The Only Way Out Is In*
1905047916 224pp £10.99 $19.95

Is There an Afterlife?
David Fontana

It will surely become a classic not only of parapsychology literature in general but also of survival literature in particular. **Radionics** Winner of the Scientific and Medical Network prize
1903816904 496pp £14.99 $19.95

Adjust Your Brain
A Practical Theory for Maximising Mental Health
Paul Fitzgerald

Fascinating, enthralling, and controversial. Paul Fitzgerald's theories of brain functioning and mental illness are certain to capture the attention of the lay person and the esteemed scientist alike. Regardless of your opinion of his ideas, this book is certain to do one thing: make you think very deeply about your perceptions, your emotions, your moods, and the very nature of what it is to be human...and about our abilities to alter these through the use of psychopharmacology. **Dr. Ryan K. Lanier,** PhD, Behavioral Pharmacologist, Johns Hopkins University School of Medicine
978-1-84694-0 224pp £11.99 $24.95